Vaughan M. Shaw.

18/2/50

WORLD REVOLUTION
IN THE CAUSE OF PEACE

WORLD
REVOLUTION
IN THE CAUSE OF
PEACE

LIONEL CURTIS

BASIL BLACKWELL
OXFORD
1949

Printed in Great Britain for BASIL BLACKWELL & MOTT, LIMITED
by A. R. MOWBRAY & CO. LIMITED, London and Oxford

TABLE OF CONTENTS

PART I

'THE AMERICAN REVOLUTION'

PART II

WORLD REVOLUTION

FORMATION OF PUBLIC OPINION

PART III

WORLD REVOLUTION

ESSENTIALS OF THE SCHEME

PART I

'THE AMERICAN REVOLUTION'

B

I

'THE AMERICAN REVOLUTION' DEFINED

IN January, 1787, Dr. Benjamin Rush of Philadelphia issued an *Address to the People of the United States* in which he wrote:

> There is nothing more common than to confound the terms of the American Revolution with those of the late American war. The American war is over; but this is far from being the case with the American Revolution. On the contrary, nothing but the first act of the great drama is closed. It remains yet to establish and perfect our new form of government; and to prepare the principles, morals, and manners of our citizens for these forms of government.

The words 'American Revolution' have a different significance for us from the meaning read into them by far-seeing Americans like Dr. Benjamin Rush. It is now of vital importance to us, and indeed to the people of Europe, to grasp what the American Revolution was, how it began, and how it was completed, for in it we may find a key to our own problem.

When the British colonies were settled in America, a Parliament elected by the people had existed for centuries in England, and had steadily increased its power. In the Act of Settlement in 1701 the principle was established once for all that the Royal Authority was itself based on an Act of Parliament responsible to the people themselves.

The British colonies were not founded in America

3

by the Government, but by corporations modelled on the guilds of the Middle Ages, or by refugees who sought in America a freedom to practise their own religion. Their legal position was established by Charters which put the legislative power into the hands of Assemblies elected by the colonists themselves. No attempt was made to represent them in the British Parliament which was too remote. None the less the British Government remained responsible for their defence and external relations, including their commerce with Europe. In return for this protection the mother country was to enjoy a monopoly of colonial trade. 'Colonies', wrote a British official in 1765, 'are only settlements made in different parts of the world for the improvement of trade.'

This idea had inspired the colonial system from 1600 onwards. In 1660 it was formulated in the Navigation Act, and was afterwards developed in more than one hundred Statutes. A tendency to value the West Indies, where sugar was raised by slave labour, above the colonies of New England was one of the disastrous results, and saddled America with the curse of slavery.

The Mercantile System, as it was called, was thus based on the principle of compact, on the common interests of communities on opposite sides of the Atlantic. Such a system was unstable, because in the course of events the interests on which it was based, changed, ceased to be common, and began to diverge. It worked only so long as France and Spain, based on the St. Lawrence and Mississippi rivers, were a standing threat to the safety of the colonies.

The moral effect of this system of compact on the colonists is the key to the history which followed the outbreak of The Seven Years' War with France. Life in the colonies under the commercial system produced a race remarkable for courage, for straight shooting, and also for readiness to take up a quarrel. But it did not make them responsible for the safety of the Empire as a whole, which was left to rest on the people of Great Britain. The colonists came to feel that that task was always done for them in the end, however much or little they might do for themselves. Hence they failed to develop the spirit which prompts a people to call out its fighting men and to keep them in the field so long as the public safety may require them. When the enemy had crossed the frontiers of their own colony and ravaged its territory, the colonial militia turned out. Their local knowledge, their marksmanship, courage, and resourcefulness combined to make them as formidable as undisciplined guerillas can be in embarrassing an organized army. But the moment the invading army moved from their own to a neighbouring colony the local militia began to disperse to their homes. Such levies were no more able to expel the French from America than were the Boer commandos able to expel the British Army from their country in the South African war. The Seven Years' War would have been greatly shortened if the task of expelling France from North American soil had not been left by the colonists to the British. It was for want of support by colonial forces that the British Army failed to complete the conquest of French territories in America by expelling the French from Louisiana, which in 1763 was ceded to Spain.

In his book *British Colonial Policy, 1754–1765*, the American historian George Louis Beer remarks that 'to a large extent the colonies neutralized the advantages arising from the British naval activity, both supplying the French colonies with the sorely needed provisions, and also furnishing a market for their produce: (p. 87).

The truth is that the colonists were unable to envisage the larger issues involved, so that, in the words of the same historian, 'What was in essence a world-wide struggle between Great Britain and France—between two different types of civilization—contracted in the narrow vision of the colonies to the dimensions of a local conflict.'

In the light of after events we can now see where the root of the trouble lay. The main struggle was between two aspects of Western civilization and two great Empires. Europe, India, and America were the theatres of that struggle. British America was divided into a number of colonies, each equipped with a democratic assembly. The issue at stake there was whether the French could conquer the far more numerous British, or whether the British could expel France once for all from American soil. The colonies themselves could never agree on any effective measures for expelling France. For among them there was no responsible authority which could take the requisite measures to assist the British Government, upon whose shoulders the burden was left to rest. It was in the provision of such a responsible authority—not, it is true, to assist the British, but to work out the destiny of an independent American nation—that in God's good time 'The American Revolution' was brought to its issue.

II

THE SEVEN YEARS' WAR AND AFTER

IN 1753, when war with France already threatened, the British Government, realizing that the incapacity of the colonial assemblies to handle the Indian tribes, which were bound to be involved in the struggle, was about to yield a terrible harvest, convoked a meeting at Albany of representatives from the colonies immediately concerned.

The Conference resolved unanimously that a union of all the colonies was necessary for their security, and adopted a masterly statement of the reasons why such a union was needed. It closed with the words: 'One principal encouragement to the French, in invading and insulting the British-American dominions, was their knowledge of our disunited state, and of our weakness arising from such want of union.' They appointed a committee to draft a plan. This plan, largely the work of Benjamin Franklin, was adopted unanimously. It provided for an executive appointed by the Crown and a legislature to be elected by the various assemblies in the colonies. This authority was to have jurisdiction over Indian affairs, and have power to raise and pay soldiers to defend the colonies and to equip vessels to guard the coasts, lakes, and rivers. For these purposes it was to have power to impose taxes.

Unhappily nothing came of this first effort to achieve union. For of the colonial commissioners who attended the Conference only those of Massachusetts were possessed of full powers. Accordingly it was provided that the plan should be first submitted to the colonies; whereupon with the same unanimity with which their representatives had approved the plan the colonial assemblies either rejected or failed to ratify it. In their hearts they knew that Britain, if left with no other choice, would assume the task of defending them. Nevertheless, this plan, though abortive, is important as the germ of the constitution under which the United States has flourished since 1787.

In 1755 the British Government resolved to provide four regiments, at the expense of the British taxpayer, to deal with the encroachments of the French and the Indians. Braddock was sent in command, and William Johnson appointed to the charge of Indian affairs. Braddock set out to attack Fort Duquesne (now Pittsburg) in Pennsylvania with the young Washington under his command; but owing to the failure of the colonists to support him he was surprised and routed by the French and Indians and himself fell mortally wounded.

In 1756, when war with France was formally declared, the colonies were in no better position to conduct their own defence. The British Government, always hard put to it to find soldiers, resorted to the expedient of making grants to colonial assemblies, proportioned to the forces they furnished. Pitt persuaded Parliament to vote £200,000 a year in payment to American colonies for defending their own territories from the French. He succeeded in bringing into the field a considerable body of colonial troops. Of these, seven-tenths were furnished by three colonies. The remaining colonies sustained a burden less than one-fourth of that assumed by the other three.

The determining action of the war was fought not in the American colonies, but in French Canada in 1759 when Wolfe defeated Montcalm on the Plains of Abraham, and took Quebec. Four years later The Seven Years' War was brought to an end by the Treaty of Paris, under which France ceded all her territories in North America to Britain, except Louisiana which was ceded to Spain. Fear of France, which had long induced the colonies to accept the mercantile system, vanished with the conquest of Canada.

In The Seven Years' War the Indian tribes had been everywhere on the side of the French. This was due to the fact that the French authority in North America was able to control trading relations with the Indians as a whole, and to see that the trade was decently conducted by French traders. The colonial assemblies of the British colonies were unable to control unscrupulous traders, who defrauded and oppressed the Indians in every way. The ink was scarcely dry on the Treaty of Paris when the frontiers of Pennsylvania and of Virginia were devastated by an Indian rising of unparalleled ferocity. The colonial militias were incapable of dealing with the situation. It was only after desperate fighting that British troops commanded by Amherst succeeded in repelling the invaders. There was now no domestic American authority capable of handling the Indians as the autocratic French Government had been able to do. The task was imposed on the British Government, and also the cost of discharging it. Anxious to reduce its forces in America it was none the less obliged to maintain a large force to deal with the Indians.

The cost of this force was estimated at £220,000 over and above the amounts voted by Parliament to support American garrisons before the war, which had doubled the national debt. It now stood at £130,000,000, the annual interest on which was £4,500,000.

The Seven Years' War had convinced Grenville, who was Chancellor of the Exchequer, that it was hopeless to expect the thirteen colonial assemblies to contribute to the cost of their own local defence. He dared not face Parliament with a proposal that the British tax-payer should assume the whole of this charge, and came to the conclusion that taxation of the colonists by Parliament itself was the only means of obtaining from them a just share of the cost of their own defence. So in 1764 he announced the intention of the government to introduce in the following year an Act requiring all legal documents to be written on paper bearing stamps purchased from the British Government. A year's notice was given in order that the colonial assemblies might render the Act unnecessary by raising the contribution for themselves. He explained to the Agents of the colonies that there was no intention of asking them to contribute to the debt incurred on account of the war or to the cost of the navy. The £45,000 was required for expenditure necessary in the future only, and in America only. If they preferred any other way of raising the money he would withdraw the Stamp Act provided the money was paid. When in February, 1765, the Agents met Grenville again, after communicating what he had said to their respective colonies, they could only argue against the measure and had no proposal to make. Franklin, who appeared as Agent for Philadelphia, urged that the demand should be made to the assembly of each colony by the Governor. 'Can you agree', asked Grenville, 'on the proportions each colony should raise?' The Agents replied in the negative and the interview was closed. This unanswered question went to the root of the matter. The problem was one which could never be solved until there was brought into existence an American Government which could undertake the expenditure required for American administrative needs.

Few of the colonists realized that the continuance of the existing situation meant saddling the British taxpayer with the cost of American administration, and the opposition aroused was such that the government was unable to collect the taxes. In 1766, Grenville having fallen from power, the Stamp Act was repealed. Pitt returned to power and went to the Lords as Earl of Chatham. He was, however, too ill to attend to business and the reins of government fell into the hands of Townshend as Chancellor of the Exchequer. The colonies under the mercantile system had always acquiesced in the payment of the light duties on imports imposed by the British Parliament. Townshend now decided to raise a contribution of £40,000 a year for colonial defence by additional duties on a number of articles, including tea.

The colonists proceeded to boycott the use of tea. Lord North, who had now succeeded Townshend at the Exchequer, repealed all the duties except that on tea which he halved. But in Boston the extremists were determined to challenge the jurisdiction of Parliament in all colonial affairs. On December 16, 1773, a party disguised as Indians boarded the tea ships of the British East India Company and emptied their cargoes into the harbour.

In April, 1775, Gage, as Governor of Massachusetts, sent a force to destroy the munitions collected by the Massachusetts assembly some twenty miles from Boston, which came into collision with a party of provincials at Lexington and sustained serious losses. Blood had been shed in New England and rebellion had broken out.

III

THE CONGRESS OF PHILADELPHIA, EFFORTS AT CONFEDERATION, WAR, AND THE DECLARATION OF INDEPENDENCE

IN June, 1774, the Massachusetts assembly invited the other colonial assemblies to send delegates to a general Congress; and on September 5, 1774, delegates from twelve colonies met at Philadelphia. When George III heard the news he exclaimed: 'The die is now cast, the colonies must either submit or triumph.' The delegates from Massachusetts, anxious to draw the southern colonies into the struggle, placed their own forces under the direction of Congress as the nucleus of an American Army. They also agreed to the appointment of George Washington, a Virginian, as Commander in Chief of the Army. This agreement to appoint a Southerner to command the combined forces of all the colonies in revolt was the most important factor in bringing the struggle to its final issue. That it made possible the creation of an American Army was much, but even that would not have availed to achieve the independence of the colonies if it had not happened that Washington proved himself supremely equal to the task of Commander in Chief.

From the outset Washington was faced by the same difficulties that British generals had met in The Seven Years' War, when they found that each colonial militia was prepared to defend the frontier of its own colony, but was not prepared to combine with the other colonial militias to end the war by driving the French out of America. The best he could do was to keep some kind of army in existence with the help of French troops and money. He was further embarrassed by the same treasonable trade with the enemy which had hampered the British in the seven years' war. In a letter dated November 7, 1780, Washington wrote to his friend Benjamin Harrison at Philadelphia:

> While our army is experiencing almost daily want, that of the enemy in New York is deriving ample supplies from a trade with the adjacent states of New York, New Jersey and Connecticut, which has by degrees become so common that it is hardly thought a crime.

One last touch was needed to complete the experience of The Seven Years' War. When the year 1781 opened with a threat of invasion from Canada, New York and Vermont were involved in a local dispute, and were actually preparing for a civil war in the probable field of Washington's campaign.

Washington realized that in order to create and maintain an American Army, there must be called into being some kind of American Government. The Congress of Philadelphia was, as its name indicates, no more than a meeting of envoys from the thirteen assemblies collected to facilitate mutual intercourse. Benjamin Franklin had also realized the impotence of a body whose resolutions had no binding effect on dissenting States, and in 1775 submitted to Congress a document, drafted on the lines of the plan he had submitted to the Conference at Albany in 1753.

It was not till 1776 that Congress found time even to consider the draft. The result was a constitution entitled 'Articles of Confederation'. It began by declaring that 'each State retains its sovereignty, freedom and independence and every power, jurisdiction and right which is not by this federation expressly delegated to the United States in Congress assembled'. But the powers, jurisdiction, and rights which States were to agree to confer upon Congress had all to be exercised through the agency of the States themselves. Congress might requisition men, money, or ships, but only from the States. The States were to promise to fulfil the requisitions, but the compact said nothing as to what was to happen if the promises were broken. These Articles of Confederation were a frank attempt to create a government between sovereign States, which 'merely defined in more precise terms the impotence of Government' (Oliver, *Life of Alexander Hamilton*, p. 102). Nevertheless, Congress was unable to induce the States to ratify even Articles of Confederation as little compelling as these, till, maddened by want of food and pay, the Pennsylvania line broke into open mutiny and threatened Congress itself. The Pennsylvanian government patched up a settlement with its own men on lines which emphasized the grievances of those from other States. The result was a mutiny in the New Jersey Contingent, which Washington suppressed by hanging two of the ringleaders.

The Articles of Confederation were not ratified by the States till February, 1781, a few months before the surrender of Yorktown.

In 1776 Washington had realized that the colonies could only win their independence with the aid of a foreign ally, and turned to their former enemy, France. But France had no interest in supporting the revolt until the Americans were pledged to secession from the British Empire. On July 4, 1776, Congress nerved itself to issue the Declaration of Independence. This was done only just in time to secure the active intervention of France, without which the revolt must have failed. It revived the failing spirit of the Americans and made it possible for Washington and a handful of devoted followers to save them from their own disorders.

In October, 1780, Congress had granted the officers half-pay for life, but the States ignored its requisitions and left the officers unpaid. Their belief in the republican cause for which they had fought was fatally shaken, and their minds were beginning to seek a cure in some form of monarchy. Colonel Nicola, an old and respected friend of Washington, undertook to convey these ideas to him and invited him in a forcible and well-written letter to assume to himself the sovereignty of the State. Once more the movement was checked by the firmness and tact of Washington's reply:

> With a mixture of surprise and astonishment, I have read with attention the sentiments you have submitted to my perusal. Be assured, sir, no occurrence in the course of the war has given me more painful sensations than your information of there being such ideas existing in the army as you have expressed and (which) I must view with abhorrence and reprehend with severity. For the present, the communication of them will rest in my own bosom, unless some further agitation of the matter shall make a disclosure necessary. I am much at a loss to conceive what part of my conduct could have given encouragement to an address which seems to me big with the greatest mischiefs that can befall my country. If I am not deceived in the knowledge of myself, you could not have found a person to whom your schemes are more disagreeable. At the same time, in justice to my own feelings, I must add that no man possesses a more sincere

wish to see justice done to the army than I do; and as far as my power and influence in a constitutional way extend, they shall be employed to the utmost of my abilities to effect it, should there be any occasion. Let me conjure you, then, if you have any regard for your country, concern for yourself or posterity, or respect for me, to banish these thoughts from your mind, and never communicate, as from yourself or anyone else, a sentiment of the like nature. (Lodge, *George Washington*, Vol. 1, pp. 329–30.)

Throughout the long struggle which belongs to military history and of which the details need not be recounted here, Washington had no greater control of American resources than could be obtained through a body of envoys each unable to pledge the State which sent him to Congress. He had had to raise the men he needed and the money to pay them by his own personal influence. The largest contingent of recruits were Irish Presbyterians, whom the commercial system and absentee landlords had driven to America inspired with an inveterate hatred of British rule. In recruiting his army Washington owed more to hatred brewed in the old country than to public spirit developed in the new.

The war was greatly prolonged by his difficulties. His final victory was made possible by French aid, and still more by the incompetence of British ministers and of the generals they sent to command the army. But most of all Americans owed their independence to the genius, heroism, and incredible patience of one man. His military achievement was consummated in 1783 by the second Treaty of Paris, in which George III acknowledged the sovereign independence of the thirteen American States.

C

IV

FAILURE OF THE ARTICLES OF CONFEDERATION

THE Americans had thus obtained the primary object for which they had fought. Peace was established, at least on paper, and Washington hastened to resign his office as Commander in Chief. In doing so he issued a circular letter to all the States, in which he reviewed the political situation, the full text of which is recorded in Marshall's *Life of Washington*, Volume V, pp. 48–65.

'An indissoluble union of the States under one federal head' was, he assured them, essential, not merely to the well-being, but also to the independence of the United States. He warned them that, unless the States suffered Congress to exercise those powers it was supposed to possess under the Constitution, there was nothing before them but anarchy and confusion. 'It is indispensable,' he added, 'to the happiness of individual States, that there should be lodged somewhere a supreme power, to regulate and govern the general concerns of the confederated republic, without which the union cannot be of long duration. . . . It is only in our united character that we are known as an Empire; that our independence is acknowledged; that our power can be regarded or our credit supported among foreign nations. The treaties of the European powers with the United States of America will have no validity on a dissolution of the Union. We shall be left nearly in a state of nature, or we may find, by our unhappy experience, that there is a natural and necessary progression from the extreme of anarchy to the extreme of tyranny; and that arbitrary power is most easily established on the ruins of liberty abused to licentiousness.'

In this circular letter to the States Washington is seen as a leader greater in peace even than he had been as a leader in war. The next five years were to verify the accuracy of his prophecy, even in details.

The Treaty of Paris was negotiated on behalf of the thirteen States by Congress acting by virtue of the Articles of Confederation. But the ink had scarcely dried on the parchment before it became clear that Congress was powerless to discharge the obligations it had assumed as the Government of the United States. It had entered into definite obligations as to the treatment of loyalists. But the loyalists were entirely in the hands of the State governments which ignored the engagements which Congress had made on their behalf. By Article IV of the Peace of Paris, the States were bound to remove every impediment to the payment of bona-fide debts owed by Americans to British subjects. In the face of this Article some of the States had passed laws cancelling such debts. Naturally the British Government declined to evacuate the posts it still held in the United States so long as these and other engagements were unfulfilled. 'Had we observed good faith on our part,' wrote Washington, 'we might have told our tale to the world with a good grace, but complaints ill become those who are found to be the first aggressors.'

It was not only with the British Government that the States were breaking faith, but with their own fellow citizens who had faced death in the ranks to win their independence, to American patriots, and also to friends in Holland, and France, who had lent Congress the money without which even Washington could not have won the war. The requisitions which Congress was entitled to make on the States under the Articles of Confederation were annually repeated and annually neglected. Between 1781 and 1786 requisitions were made amounting in all to $15,870,987. To meet these requisitions no more than $2,450,803 were paid by the States.

This failure of the States to discharge their clear obligations had compelled Congress to borrow large sums from their own citizens, from France, and from sympathizers in Holland. Interest due on these debts had been partly met by a fresh loan negotiated in Holland after the war, but when this was spent Congress defaulted. Continental securities sank to one-tenth of their nominal value. Hence the phrase still current in American slang 'not worth a Continental'. As Washington wrote in October, 1785, 'from the high ground on which we stood, we are descending into the vale of confusion and darkness'.

In a letter dated June 27, 1786, Jay, who was now in charge of foreign affairs, wrote to Washington that the authority, not merely of Congress, but of the States themselves was threatened with dissolution.

'Your sentiments', replied Washington, 'that our affairs are drawing rapidly to a crisis accord with my own. . . . I do not conceive we can exist long as a nation, without lodging somewhere a power which will pervade the whole union in as energetic a manner as the authority of the State governments extends over the several States.

. . . Requisitions are a perfect nullity, where thirteen sovereign independent, disunited States, are in the habit of discussing, and refusing or complying with them at their option. Requisitions are actually little better than a jest, and a by-word throughout the land. . . . I am told that even respectable characters speak of a monarchial form of government without horror. From thinking proceeds speaking, thence to acting is often but a single step. . . . What a triumph for the advocates of despotism, to find that we are incapable of governing ourselves.'

The vast territories west of the colonies which the first Treaty of Paris had secured to Britain in 1763, were now transferred by another Treaty of Paris in 1783 to the victorious Americans. Washington foresaw their importance at a time when few were giving the matter a thought. Their settlement and development depended on the building of canals to connect the States with the unpeopled lands on the banks of the Mississippi and its tributaries. As the States and Congress were alike incapable of handling this constructive task, Washington founded a joint stock company to build the canals. He foresaw that when these lands were settled the easiest course for the settlers would be to float their produce down the Mississippi, the mouths of which were in the hands of Spain. But he also saw that 'a habit of trade' with a foreign power might lead these western lands when settled to break off from the Union.

To discuss this and other difficulties with the States that had shown interest in the enterprise he arranged for them to meet at Mount Vernon in March, 1785. There the need of a uniform currency, of customs duties, and for better co-operation between the States came under discussion. It was finally decided to propose to all the thirteen States to send delegates to Annapolis late in the following year (1786) to discuss the whole economic situation.

Before this date arrived, the currency collapsed, the taxpayers were led by an Irish ex-officer, Major Shay, in armed rebellion against their own government in Massachusetts. Disputes with Spain about the free navigation of the Mississippi had come to a head. Jay advised Congress to close the river for twenty-five years. The southern States threatened if this were done to secede and return to British allegiance, while the New England States made the same threats unless the river was closed. New Jersey, Pennsylvania, and Rhode Island sided with the south.

Such was the atmosphere of chaos in which the convention met at Annapolis. Of the thirteen States only five attended the convention, but of these one was New York, which sent Alexander Hamilton, Washington's aide, who had led the final attack on Cornwallis in Yorktown. Hamilton convinced the others that the only remedy for the economic evils they were facing would be found in constitutional changes beyond their commissions. The political problem was the key to the functional problem. They agreed on an address to the States drafted by Hamilton which recommended that:

> The States by which they have been respectively delegated would concur themselves, and use their endeavours to procure the concurrence of the other States in the appointment of commissioners to meet at

Philadelphia on the second Monday in May next, to take into consideration the situation of the United States, to devise such further provisions as shall appear to them necessary to render the constitution of the Federal Government *adequate to the exigencies of the Union.* (Oliver, *The Life of Alexander Hamilton*, pp. 137–42.)

V

THE PHILADELPHIA CONVENTION OF 1787 AND EFFECTIVE FEDERATION

SO long as the war lasted men of action with a sense of realities, of whom Hamilton was one, were serving in the army. The political situation remained in the hands of men who knew how to talk and tried to solve practical problems by phrases. When peace had released from the army men who had handled facts under Washington, and thus developed a sense of realities, the situation began to change. The address issued by the small convention at Annapolis was a result of this change. In all the States but Rhode Island the politicians were now thoroughly frightened, and agreed to the proposed convention. On May 14, 1787, their delegates met in the State House in Philadelphia where eleven years before the Declaration of Independence had been signed. Washington was unanimously elected to preside. The State politicians had convinced him that public opinion in the thirteen States would refuse to accept any surrender of State sovereignty. He opened the proceedings by telling the delegates that they were not there to follow public opinion, but to tell the public what, having won the war, they must still do to win the peace.

It is too probable that no plan we propose will be adopted. Perhaps another dreadful conflict is to be sustained. If to please the people, we offer what we our-

selves disapprove, how can we afterwards defend our
work? Let us raise a standard to which the wise and
honest can repair. The event is in the hands of God.

From the outset the discussions were shrouded in
secrecy and closely guarded. Official records were
confined to bare minutes of the resolutions. In 1830
Madison, who had filled the office of American
President, recorded his belief that no constitution
would ever have been adopted if the debates had been
held in public. He himself, however, had kept a careful
note of the discussions which was only published in
1840. Some eight other delegates also made notes
which were published in after years. In *The Great
Rehearsal*, published in London by the Cresset Press in
1948, Carl van Doren has compiled an admirable
account of the discussions from these materials. His
lucid narrative need not be repeated here. The final
result of these discussions can be seen in the Constitution of the United States signed by the delegates on
September 17, 1787, which shows how a resolute
majority had followed the lead which Washington
gave in his opening words. No little courage was
needed, for the politicians had been at work trying to
sterilize the convention in advance.

The Annapolis Convention had called on the States
to send delegates to Philadelphia 'to devise such further
provisions as shall appear to them necessary to render
the constitution of the Federal Government adequate
to the exigencies of the Union'. On February 21,
1787, Congress did its best to emasculate this forthright
reference by passing a resolution that 'it is expedient
that on the second Monday in May next a Convention
of delegates who shall have been appointed by the

several States be held at Philadelphia for the sole
and express purpose of *revising The Articles of Confederation*
and reporting to Congress and the several legislatures
such alterations and provisions therein as shall when
agreed to in Congress and confirmed by the States
render the federal constitution adequate to the
exigencies of Government and the preservation of the
Union'.

The intention of Congress was to confine the
convention to a mere revision of the Articles of
Confederation. Some delegates tried to do this, but
as the debates proceeded the Resolution of Congress
was first ignored and then forgotten. The only State
not represented at Philadelphia was Rhode Island.
In the end delegates from the other twelve signed a
document which began with the words:

> We the people of the United States, in order to form a
> more perfect Union, establish justice, ensure domestic
> tranquillity, provide for the common defence, promote
> general welfare, and secure the blessings of liberty to
> ourselves and our Posterity, do ordain and establish this
> *Constitution* for the United States of America.

This Constitution provided that power to levy and
collect taxes, pay debts, provide for the common
defence and welfare of the United States, to raise
loans, regulate commerce between the States with
Indian tribes and foreign governments, regulate
naturalization, bankruptcy, and weights and measures,
coin money, establish post offices and roads, control
copyright and patents, constitute federal courts,
suppress pirates and enforce international law, declare
war, raise an army and navy, suppress insurrections
and control the federal capital, and make laws neces-

sary for carrying these powers into effect should be vested in a Congress of the United States consisting of a Senate and Houses of Representatives. The Senate was to consist of two senators from each State chosen by its legislature, the Lower House of members chosen by the electors of the several States. Executive power was to vest in a President elected for four years by an electoral college, which came to mean in practice that the President is directly elected by the whole American electorate. The judicial power of the United States was vested in one Supreme Court and such inferior courts as Congress might establish.

The last article (VII) provided that:

> The ratification of the Conventions of nine States, shall be sufficient for the establishment of this Constitution between the States so ratifying the same.

This article is proof that the convention had ended by following Washington's advice to ignore what the State politicians said was 'public opinion' and to 'raise a standard to which the wise and honest can repair'.

In the course of the debates some delegates had begun to doubt whether the State politicians were right in asserting that public opinion was opposed to any merger of the State sovereignties in the United States. On June 12th, Madison voiced these doubts when he said:

> No member of the Convention could say what the opinion of his Constituents were at this time; much less could he say what they would think if possessed of the information and lights possessed by the members here; and still less what would be their way of thinking six or twelve months hence. We ought to consider what was right and necessary in itself for the attainment of a proper government.

His last sentence clearly re-echoed the advice with
which Washington had opened the convention. When
the convention adjourned to celebrate July 4th,
Hamilton had left for New York. On July 3rd he wrote
to Washington that he had talked to a number of
persons on the way who were afraid the convention

from a fear of shocking the popular opinion will not
go far enough. . . . Men in office are indeed taking all
possible pains to give an unfavourable opinion of the
convention; but the current seems to be running strongly
the other way.

The State legislatures had assumed that a Constitution for a United States could only be brought into
operation by their own approval. By Article VII they
were boldly by-passed and acceptance was made to
depend on *ad hoc* conventions directly elected by the
primary voters in each State—a frank appeal to public
opinion itself over the heads of the State politicians.
The reactionary view had been strongly voiced by the
smaller States, especially by the delegates from Delaware, New Jersey, and Georgia, who were bound by
instructions from their State legislatures. As Madison
had said on June 29th, that view was fatal to the
freedom and peace of America.

The same causes which have rendered the old world
the theatre of incessant wars, and have banished liberty
from the face of it, would soon produce the same effects
here.

In the end, however, the larger States, led by
Virginia, prevailed in securing a Constitution, under
which North America was destined to become the
greatest field of peace and freedom in the world.

Within four months its publication was followed by results that surprised politicians no less than the re-election of President Truman in 1948. On December 7th Delaware, on December 18th New Jersey, and on January 2nd Georgia had unanimously approved the Constitution in conventions elected by the voters in those States. Their example was quickly followed by others. On June 21, 1788, the Constitution was approved by the ninth State and came into operation. An overwhelming majority of Americans had shown that they preferred freedom and peace to their State sovereignties. Washington was elected President by universal consent, and appointed Hamilton as Treasurer. The fact that the new contrivance worked was largely due to the patience, devotion, and capacity which both of them showed in the first administration. It was also due to the experience which members of Congress had gained in the State legislatures. That it worked was a great surprise to most observers in Europe, and to some in America. That it did so accounts for the momentous fact that within the course of a century the thirteen founder States were joined by thirty-five others. These forty-eight States, united as one nation, had become the greatest power on earth.

VI

THE AMERICAN REVOLUTION COMPLETED
BY CIVIL WAR

WE must not, however, leap to the conclusion that because the Federal Constitution had been adopted and worked it had brought to fruition what Dr. Benjamin Rush had called 'The American Revolution'. The mercantile system had saddled the States with the curse of slavery. As Madison told the convention, the great division of interests in the United States did not lie between the large and small States but between the southern and northern; between those which had or did not have slaves. Delegates from the north had even argued that provision for abolishing slavery should be incorporated in the Constitution. In the light of after events the convention has been blamed because it did not forestall the civil war which nearly destroyed the Union in 1860 by facing up to the issue in 1787. To one who has lived in a country where the colour bar is sanctioned by law, it is hard to believe that a cancer as deeply embedded as the slave system was in the southern States could be removed except by an operation involving the shedding of blood. Tradition has it that as he signed the report of the convention on September 17, 1787, Washington remarked: 'Should the States reject this excellent constitution . . . the next will be drawn in blood'. In effect it was.

The Constitution of 1787 was written in the hope

that under the federal system free and slave States could exist in one Commonwealth side by side. The Federal Government was responsible for the organization of new States in the vast territories of the west. To which of the systems were new States to belong, to the slave or to the free? Experience proved that territory organized as a free State was practically closed to colonization from the slave States, and that territory organized as a slave State was closed to colonists bred under the free conditions of the north.

The first sign of the gathering storm was raised in 1820 by a proposal to admit Missouri as a slave State. Jefferson, who had drafted the Declaration of Independence, wrote:

> This momentous question, like a fire-bell in the night awakened and filled me with terror. I considered it at once the knell of the Union.

For the time the issues were compromised by an arrangement which admitted Missouri as a slave State, but also provided that its southern boundary (36° 30′) was to be taken as the frontier between slave and free States in the vast territory which had been purchased from Spain under the name of Louisiana. The compromise merely postponed the issue till in the territory of Kansas two opposing governments were established, one by settlers from the north as a free State, the other by settlers from the south as a slave State. But as the south controlled the Senate and the north the House, nothing could be settled and Kansas lapsed into civil war. In 1856 the Democratic party was able to elect the President and regain control of the House. The north, meanwhile, was finding its leader in Abraham

Lincoln, who in 1860 was elected President. The south had now lost control of the Federal Government, and resolved to secede.

The Constitution framed in 1787 had scotched but not killed the contractual principle upon which the Articles of Confederation had been based. To the south the institution of slavery was dearer than that of the American Republic, and they nursed a theory which struck at the root of the Union. Hayne of South Carolina had declared in 1830:

> Before the Constitution each State was an independent sovereignty, possessing all the rights and powers appertaining to independent nations. . . . The true nature of the Federal Constitution is a compact to which the States are parties.

The southern States thus reverted to the theory that the Union had been based on a compact between sovereign States, and not, as Hamilton had urged, on the individual dedication of the citizens to the United States. If, as the south argued, the authority of the Union was derived from the sovereignty of the States, they, by virtue of their sovereignty, could recall it.

They were faced, however, by a leader who saw in the Constitution, not a compact, but a creed, and declared that

> the Union gave each of the States whatever independence or liberty it has; the Union is older than any of the States, and in fact it created them as States.

In his creed the ultimate obedience of Americans was due neither to the States nor to the Federal Government, but to the United States of America, from which both State and Federal Governments derived their powers. Lincoln realized that the point was reached when a State, be it Commonwealth or Despotism, can survive only by making its ultimate claim on the devotion of such of its members as desire that it should survive. He must call on such members to exact obedience by force from those who denied the authority of the Union and meant to destroy it. The ultimate issue which divided Americans was not their preference for freedom or slavery, but the question which each must answer for himself, whether their final allegiance was due to the government of their State or to that of the United States of America.

These claims made by Lincoln met with a response strangely different from that which had been given to Washington. That greatest of leaders had been left to fill up his army with men not bred in America, and to pay them from revenues which had not been earned there. But now when his work was threatened with destruction enough Americans were ready to pour out their blood and treasure to preserve the Union. The civil war is estimated to have cost not far from $10,000,000,000 and 1,000,000 lives. No leader comparable to Washington was found to direct the armies of the north. The north's ultimate victory, after many defeats, was the product, not of a military genius backed by a handful of devoted followers, but of the devotion of American citizens, who for three generations had elected a President and Congress and had paid the taxes which the government they elected imposed on them. The result has proved that it is not by self-interest that Commonwealths are knit, but by a sense of obligation which, unless it is exercised, withers away and flourishes only in so far as it is called into action.

D

Under a system which imposed on Americans the real burdens of statehood patriotism grew as fast as it had languished under systems which failed to impose them.

What Dr. Benjamin Rush in 1787 had called 'The American Revolution' was thus, in fact, completed eighty years later. At last the task of keeping the peace was transferred once for all from a number of sovereign States to the shoulders of the people themselves by a Constitution finally based not on compact but on what Lincoln described as the dedication of its citizens to the United States. Once for all it became the government of the people for the people by the people. Thenceforward the North American continent became the greatest field of peace that the world had seen.

On November 24, 1787, James Wilson used the following words to the convention which brought Pennsylvania under the Constitution:

> To frame a government for a single city or state, is a business both in its importance and facility, widely different to the task entrusted to the Federal Convention, whose prospects were extended not only to thirteen independent and sovereign States, some of which in territorial, jurisdiction, population and resource, equal the most respectable nations of Europe, but likewise to innumerable States yet unformed, to myriads of citizens who in future States shall inhabit the vast uncultivated regions of the continent. The duties of that body, therefore, were not limited to local or partial considerations, but to the formation of a plan commensurate with a great and valuable portion of the globe.

In the last words that William Pitt uttered in public he declared that 'England had saved herself by her exertions, and would save Europe by her example'.

As Abraham Lincoln lay dying in the hour of his achievement he might with justice have said that America had saved herself by her exertions. And might he not have foretold that America would yet save Europe and the world by her example?

VII

RECAPITULATION
HOW THE AMERICAN PEACE WAS WON

IN the light of the facts narrated in the previous chapters we can see that to thoughtful Americans like Dr. Benjamin Rush 'The American Revolution' meant more than acquisition by the thirteen States of their independence. This independence had had the effect of bringing Americans face to face with the facts governing the issues of peace and war.

The facts had proved beyond dispute the incompetence of thirteen sovereign governments to maintain peace between themselves or to avert the standing menace of foreign invasion. The American Revolution had only ended when it was decided once for all, first by the Constitution of 1787 and finally by the victory of the north in the civil war, that responsibility for keeping the peace of North America must be transferred from the sovereign governments to the electorate of the United States. Since the time of Lincoln American voters, when electing the President and Congress, have known that the issues of peace and war rested finally on themselves. We have only to think of the last four elections in the U.S.A. to see how they face that responsibility. Especially was this so in the presidential election of 1948 when both parties agreed to treat foreign affairs as above and outside party politics. The effect of responsibility in bringing a vast democracy to face unpalatable facts and profound spiritual issues has never been better exemplified. The result has been that though the U.S.A. was involved with the rest of the world in war, not a shot was fired, not a bomb fell, on the North American continent. How different the case would have been if in 1914 and in 1939 the issues of peace or war had been in the hands of forty-eight sovereign States.

On September 15, 1787, in the closing session of the Philadelphia Convention, Randolph, Governor of Virginia, supported by Mason, a delegate from that State, moved that the draft Constitution should be first submitted to State conventions, and then brought back to Philadelphia to consider the amendments proposed. Charles Pinckney, delegate for South Carolina, replied that while he had his own objections to the draft

> Apprehending the danger of a general confusion, *and an ultimate decision by the sword*, he should give the plan his support.

The motion which Randolph and Mason had moved was then rejected by unanimous vote.

Pinckney's lead followed by this vote shows how the decision to go forward with a draft, with all the details of which none of the delegates were agreed, was moved by the feeling that nothing else could save America from another outbreak of war. The convention had realized that until the spectre of war was laid, no other major problem could be solved.

We can thus see the amazing change which had taken place in the attitude of Americans between the first Peace of Paris in 1763 and the second in 1783, which granted the States their independence and so threw them on their own resources. For twenty years the politics of the country had been in the hands of men not in direct contact with facts, who thought that the problems by which they were faced could be solved by wishful thinking and phrases. The War of Independence was prolonged thereby, and was only won in the end by the genius of Washington and his devoted followers in the army. The peace released these men who were in touch with the facts and began to take the situation in hand. Their long experience of facts had given them an insight into politics which found expression in the Constitution of 1787 and, later on, in papers of Hamilton, Madison, and Jay, published under the title of *The Federalist* in New York. These followers of Washington saw that all they had fought for would be lost unless a real government could be established for the United States, strong enough to restrain the States themselves from mutual conflict over boundaries and tariffs, and to prevent the foreign invasion which was certain to follow a civil war.

They had realized that the thirteen sovereign States were incompetent to prevent war, which would only be averted if the function of keeping the peace was transferred from these sovereign governments to the people themselves. They saw that this transfer could not be made by any revision of The Articles of Confederation. They ignored the reference that Congress tried to impose on them, and drafted a new Constitution which confined the States to their local affairs, and remitted the task of keeping the peace to an executive and legislature elected by the people themselves.

We can now see that this change could not be made little by little, but only when the electorate were asked to take or refuse by their votes a document in which the nature of the change required was defined in detail as well as in outline. The authors of this Constitution realized that whatever the State politicians might say, the people at large were ready to merge the State sovereignties in the sovereignty of the United States in order to ensure peace. The amazing rapidity with which the electorates endorsed the Constitution proved how much more they valued security against war than their State sovereignties.

All this shows us what Americans like Dr. Benjamin Rush meant by 'The American Revolution'. To them it meant incomparably more than independence of Great Britain. It meant winning the peace, a task not finally accomplished till the victory of the north had established once for all the principle that the Constitution was not based on a compact between sovereign States, but on the dedication of every American citizen to one United States of America.

VIII

THE AMERICAN REVOLUTION AND THE IDEAL OF A WORLD REVOLUTION COMPARED

ON October 22, 1787, Benjamin Franklin wrote to Ferdinand Grand, his friend in Paris:

> I send you enclos'd the propos'd new Federal Constitution for these States. I was engag'd 4 months of the last Summer in the Convention that form'd it. It is now sent by Congress to the several States for their Confirmation. *If it succeeds, I do not see why you might not in Europe carry the Project of good Henry the 4th into Execution, by forming a Federal Union and One Grand Republick of all its different States and Kingdoms, by means of a like Convention, for we had many Interests to reconcile.*

The foresight of Franklin will be seen if in the *Address to the United States*, which Dr. Benjamin Rush published in January, 1787, we change the word 'American' into the word 'World'. It will then run as follows:

> There is nothing more common than to confound the terms of the World Revolution with those of the late World War. The World War is over; but this is far from being the case with the World Revolution. On the contrary, nothing but the first act of the great drama is closed. It remains yet to establish and perfect our new form of government; and to prepare the principles, morals and manners of our citizens for these forms of Government.

We have here an accurate statement of the situation which the world is facing to-day.

During the War of Independence the protagonists of State sovereignty had maintained that the Articles of Confederation must be changed little by little, until by imperceptible steps Congress was converted from an assembly of envoys into a government that could govern, because its authority was drawn from the taxpayers themselves. No progress was made on this policy which prolonged the war and, when it was won, plunged America into bankruptcy and chaos. Politicians continued to insist on the 'inevitability of gradualness'. Organic union between the States must be approached by gradual and imperceptible steps. In fact, this policy was treated by the State politicians as Grattan treated Pitt's proposal for settling Anglo-Irish relations as an 'incipient and creeping union'. It ended by arousing what Grattan had called an 'insuperable jealousy, a fever of distrust in the minds of those it was meant to conciliate'. It is worth noting that in recent years this same policy of a gradual and imperceptible approach to a closer union between the sovereign States of the British Commonwealth has met with the same results. The proposal of Australia to establish a permanent secretariat composed of representatives from the governments concerned has resulted in driving other Dominion Governments in the opposite direction. In the spring of 1946, when Dominion ministers met the British Prime Minister, they agreed on nothing more than that the Imperial Conference should be allowed to lapse. The attempt to hold another Imperial Conference in 1948 was due to the public agitation which the attempt made in 1946 to liquidate the Conference provoked.

In 1787 the functional approach had signally failed

to lift the fear of another dreadful calamity which oppressed the public mind. It is now clear that what lifted that fear from American minds was the new Constitution which electorates were asked to accept or reject by their votes. The functional approach had failed, and was bound to fail, to banish the fear of war which distracted the public mind and demoralized public policy. Nothing short of a new Constitution, which put the responsibility squarely on the shoulders of the people themselves, could avail to banish that fear. It must always be held in mind that before 1787 State electorates could not realize that prevention of war was the question they had to face in casting their votes. But under the new Constitution they came to realize at Presidential elections that this was the ultimate question they had to face. The last four Presidential elections have shown how the American electorate have risen to that responsibility.

The Philadelphia Convention had shown its greatness in grasping the fact that it was not the faults of men, but an obsolete and defective system that imperilled the peace of America. Leaders like Washington, Roosevelt, or Churchill can save their peoples from the worst results of a wrong system, though at infinite cost in lives, treasure, and moral values. The League of Nations Association are for ever claiming that the League would have prevented war had statesmen of first-rate ability been in charge of the States that composed it. In doing so they pronounce the final condemnation of their own handiwork. A system which can only maintain the peace of the world so long as it is in the hands of first-rate men is a standing danger to peace. It is self-condemned, for no system has a right to count on an unbroken succession of first-rate leaders to see that it works. The only systems to be trusted are those which continue to maintain peace when run by leaders of average ability. Experience has proved that the Constitution of 1787 is such a system. Its authors had grasped that the root of the evil was not in the men, but in the system itself, and could only be removed by a revolution. The Constitution in 1787 was the instrument of that revolution which was only completed by the civil war.

IX

FAILURE OF THE FUNCTIONAL APPROACH TO REMOVE FEAR OF WAR

FROM the facts cited in the previous chapters readers may see how far the situation which Europe and the world is now facing resembles the situation which after 1783 the sovereign States in America were facing in their more limited field. The second world war came to an end in 1945; yet since then the victorious nations have trembled in fear of war between themselves. They cannot even settle the terms upon which peace is to be made with the vanquished. In the world at large, as in the U.S.A. after 1783, society hovers on the verge of chaos and bankruptcy. Their attempts to correct the vast dislocations made by the war have signally failed. In their first attempt they have followed the example set when the American States adopted the Articles of Confederation, and entrusted that assembly of diplomats with the task of maintaining 'collective security'. The League of Nations which had failed in the task was reconstructed as the United Nations Organization. Both were based on the same principle as the Articles of Confederation, that is to say on a compact between sovereign States, which in terms maintained their sovereignty. On November 30, 1946, Brierly, then Professor of International Law at Oxford, in his Henry Sidgwick Memorial Lecture at Cambridge, said:

> We must realize that what we have done is to exchange a scheme which might or might not have worked for one

which cannot work, and that instead of limiting the sovereignty of States we have actually extended the sovereignty of the Great Powers, the only states whose sovereignty is still a formidable reality in the modern world.

That events have justified Brierly's criticism was recognized by Mr. Bevin himself when he told the House of Commons on December 9, 1948, that he would not

comment on another International institution, the United Nations, which was giving all of us at the moment very grave concern about its effectiveness. The United Nations was giving grave concern whether it was going to face the problem.

In its issue of December 17, 1948, that sober organ of the Evangelical Churches opens its first page with this comment:

At last the teeth of U.N.O. have gnashed themselves to a standstill; their noisy session has clattered to its close. The security Council lingers on; but the General Assembly is adjourned until April Fool's Day. For three months the Assembly has been speaking in half a hundred languages and has said nothing in all of them. Untransacted business hangs festooned about it—while millions—while hundreds of millions—suffer and are afraid.

The Record here speaks for the ordinary man. U.N.O., like the Articles of Confederation, is no more than an attempt to create a government based on compact between sovereign States which 'merely defines in more precise terms the impotence of Government'.

Its title reveals the faith of its founders in the virtue

of words—the United Nations whose debates expose and accentuate disunion, the Security Council the focus of danger to peace, and its record of failure dated from Lake Success.

On looking back to 1787 it is clear that the authors of the Constitution had seen how to end the American Revolution, because they grasped the paramount object to achieve, which was to remove the fear of war which was poisoning the air of America. We in 1949 shall be able to see how to achieve the World Revolution if we too realize that our primary task is to remove the fear of war which distracts not Europe only, but the world at large. We shall then be conscious that this can only be done by transferring the task of preventing war from the hands of sovereign governments and placing it squarely on the shoulders of the people themselves. We shall also see that this task cannot be placed on the shoulders of peace-loving peoples except by their own act in accepting a measure which places the burden once for all on themselves. In order to do this their leaders must place before them a measure designed for the purpose to accept or reject.

This was the work that the Philadelphia Convention did with little to guide them but a clear grasp that the fear of war must be laid before anything else could be done. With us it is otherwise. We have for our guidance the experience of the Philadelphia Convention, and precedents in Canada, Australia, and South Africa, as to the path to be followed. This cannot be done until the nations concerned have sent delegates to such meetings as took place at Philadelphia in 1787, and in Canada in 1864, Australia in 1900, and South Africa in 1909.

The first point to notice is how quickly the fear of war subsided when the American people had accepted and brought into operation the Constitution framed in 1787. Exactly the same happened in South Africa when the union of its four colonies came into operation in 1910. Nothing short of a definite decision on the part of electorates, such as that made in 1787 and in 1910, will end the fear of intestine war, exposing the participants to foreign aggression. It cannot be ended by the 'functional approach', by 'a creeping and incipient union' which presently arouses 'an insuperable jealousy'. This, in truth, is the one merit of the attempt which is always made in these cases to solve the problem by gradual and imperceptible steps, in the faith that one day the peoples concerned will wake up to find that the problem has been solved for them overnight. In fact, they awake to find the menace and fear of impending war steadily growing. Public opinion then becomes vocal and so urgent that national leaders are at last compelled to come together, as did those of the thirteen sovereign States in America, and tell the electorate what must be done to remove the fear of war.

PART II

WORLD REVOLUTION

FORMATION OF PUBLIC OPINION

X

SERVICEMEN AT WORK ON WINNING THE PEACE

WE were now at last in sight of just such a meeting and we owed it to one whose leadership in the second war raised him to a position in the world comparable to that which Washington filled in America after he had won the War of Independence.

. As in America the preliminary work was done by men who had taken an active part in the war. In 1942, when forces from all the united nations were stationed in Britain, the War Office started what were called 'Leave groups' in Oxford. Every week from seventy to eighty men and women in uniform, of all ranks, from all the allied forces, were gathered for a week in Balliol College to hear lectures. It was soon found that one subject upon which their minds were set was how to prevent a third war. For three years, till the war was won, each group devoted a number of hours in its week to working out a policy for winning the peace. The most active sections were those from the American, Canadian, and Australian forces who understood the working of federal institutions. More than 3,000 people in uniform took part in this work. As the war was ending their proceedings and conclusions were recorded in a book called *World War; its Cause and Cure*, published by the Oxford University Press in 1945. It was afterwards translated into French with an introduction by Professor Rappard, recommending it to readers in Switzerland, France, Belgium, and Quebec, and was published in Neuchâtel under the title of *Fédération ou Guerre*.

An American edition was published by Putnams at the instance of a Committee organized by Mr. Justice Owen Roberts and Professor Einstein, in a jacket giving the names of the Committee, with a preface recommending it to American readers. A Norse translation was published in Stockholm by Ljus under the title of *Varldskrig eller Varldsfred*. In 1947 the British Control Commission in Germany published 5,000 copies of a German translation under the title of *Weltkrig*, which was sold off within four weeks.

In England the book was read by members of Rotary Clubs and others. Meetings to discuss it rapidly disclosed the fact that ordinary citizens were prepared to merge their national sovereignty in an international union when convinced that nothing less would arrest the drift to a third war. Public opinion on this vital question was moving ahead of the views which prevailed in Whitehall. As in America in 1787–1788 public opinion had moved ahead of the views held by the State politicians. That this should happen is in the nature of things. The life of politicians is devoted to framing, passing, and administering laws, all based on the assumption that they do so by virtue of the sovereign power of their national government. Inevitably they come to feel that their national sovereignty is part of the order of nature, and that its maintenance intact is the first and last duty that representatives owe their electorate. They are apt to forget that ordinary people, who do not make and administer laws but only obey them, do not think of their national sovereignty as the end-all and be-all of civilized life. But every day and every hour they know how war has disordered their lives. Politicians are slow to realize that by ordinary men the maintenance of peace is felt as an object which transcends the maintenance of national sovereignty.

A national government is a fortress of sovereignty. Its walls are guarded by politicians, a garrison changed to some extent at every election. But inside those walls at the centre of the fortress is a keep, the garrison of which is not changed by elections, but here, at any rate, devote their whole lives to the service and maintenance of the national government. They advise their masters the politicians regardless of party, and whether their advice is taken or rejected obey their instructions with exemplary skill and devoted loyalty. Less in touch with public opinion, permanent officials are even more disposed than politicians to regard the maintenance of national sovereignty as the end and object of all policy. They are slower, even than politicians, to perceive when the common people are beginning to feel the price of peace is willingness to merge their national sovereignty in an international sovereignty. To civil servants such an idea is as dangerous a heresy as questioning the authority of the Church is to the Jesuit order. It is no exaggeration to say that any proposal to merge the national sovereignty in an international sovereignty would seem to permanent officials more dangerous than communism, if only because they know that in this country communism has not the slightest chance of gaining control of the government.

XI

THE MOVEMENT OF PUBLIC OPINION
BEGINS TO AFFECT MINISTERS

AS the war came to a close the growing belief that
maintenance of national sovereignties was incompatible with the maintenance of peace began to
penetrate to government circles. The late Mr. Jan
Hofmeyr, deputy leader of the South African Government, who had spent some time in Europe, returned to
South Africa by air. On landing at Maritzburg on
November 13, 1945, he spoke as follows:

I have been speaking of South Africa's problems. For us,
of course, they are difficult enough—they tend to fill our
horizon—but don't let us forget the bigger issues at stake;
don't let us be unmindful of the wider obligations that rest
upon us all as citizens of the world.

South Africa after all cannot be really prosperous unless
world prosperity is restored. South Africa will be drawn
helplessly to destruction, if civilization goes under, as well
it may.

I do not regard the world's immediate problems, political
and economic, great though they are, as insoluble. We must
not let ourselves be disheartened by the magnitude of those
problems as they present themselves to us to-day. Let us
not forget that we have just come to the end of the most
convulsive war in human history—that time and patience
are necessary for the disturbances it has set up to spend
themselves.

.   .   .   .   .

Despite the failure of the Council of Foreign Ministers
I have little doubt that the present political tension will be
resolved. I am sure also that, albeit painfully and at great

54

cost of human life and suffering, Europe will win its way back to a state of economic well-being.

But I do view with profound disquiet the long-range possibilities of disaster for humanity.

The development of the atomic bomb carries with it as a consequence that a war in which it is used on both sides will send our civilization reeling into the night. It is, therefore, of the profoundest significance for us all that such a war should be prevented. The San Francisco Conference applied itself to the problem of world security. I fear that the development of the atomic bomb has rendered the work of that conference, successful though it was in relation to the circumstances then prevailing, now largely out of date.

From the purely political point of view, I can see no way of saving humanity from destruction in the altered circumstances created by the atomic bomb, short of the creation of a form of world government, which will be more than a League of Sovereign States, but will be responsible to a truly international electorate. That means, of course, the substantial impairment of the concept of national sovereignty, and I need not tell you that so far even the atomic bomb has not availed to shake the nations into willingness to accept a solution of that kind.

The truth of the matter is that man's scientific and technical progress has outstripped his moral and spiritual advance.

On November 22, 1945, Mr. Anthony Eden startled the House of Commons by saying:

Let me come to what seems to me to be the fundamentals of this problem. The truth is that by the discovery of this atomic energy science has placed us several laps ahead of every present phase of international political development, and unless we can catch up politically to the point we have reached in science, and thus command the power which at present threatens us, we are all going to be blown to smithereens. I think that Mr. Byrnes, the United States Secretary of State, put it quite well at Charleston when he said the civilized world cannot survive an atomic war, and I agree entirely with the Prime Minister that no set of rules will enable us to survive a future war when this weapon is latent for use. I agree, too, that no safeguards by themselves will provide an effective guarantee. They have to be accompanied by the acceptance of the rule of law amongst the nations. It is something more than a hundred years ago that Castlereagh first conceived the idea of making progress in diplomacy by contact. He was on the right lines, but he failed. After the last war the nations tried again, by the League, to make another effort more in conformity with the developments that had taken place in the intervening period, and they failed, and during this war we at San Francisco tried again, and have sought to lay the foundations of a new world order.

The truth is that all the inventions of recent years have tended the same way, to narrow the world, to bring us closer together, and, therefore, to intensify the shock and sharpen the reactions before the shock absorbers are ready. Every succeeding scientific discovery makes greater nonsense of old-time conceptions of sovereignty, and yet it is not the least use our deluding ourselves, any more than Mr. Byrnes did in his Charleston speech. It is yet true that national sentiment is still as strong as ever, and here and there it is strengthened by this further complication, the different conceptions of forms of government and different conceptions of what words mean, words like 'freedom' and 'democracy'. So, despite some stirrings, the world has not, so far, been ready to abandon, or even really to modify, its old conceptions of sovereignty. But there have been some stirrings. There was the Briand plan after the last war for the Federation of Europe, which my right hon. Friend revived in another form in what he said in Brussels the other day, about the new unity of the European family. In the darkest hour of 1940 there was the offer made to France by my right hon. Friend the Member for Woodford (Mr. Churchill), on behalf of the Coalition Government, and there were the various suggestions made between the United States and ourselves. Now atomic energy has come to enforce the call for something more, because the world family is smaller to-day than was the European family at the end of the last war. I have thought much on this question of atomic energy both before and since that bomb burst on Nagasaki, and *for the life of me I have been unable to see, and am still unable to see, any final solution which will make the world safe for atomic power, save that we all abate our present ideas of sovereignty.*

We have got somehow to take the sting out of nationalism. We cannot hope to do so at once, but we ought to start working for it now, and that, I submit, should be the first duty of the United Nations. We should make up our minds where we want to go. In this respect I know where I want to go. I want to get a world in which relations between the nations can be transformed in a given period of time—we cannot do it in a short period—as the relations between this country and Scotland and Wales have been transformed.

The world was even more startled when on the following day, November 23, 1945, Mr. Bevin, speaking as Foreign Secretary, said to the House of Commons:

... I agree with the right hon. Gentleman that the coming of the atomic bomb and other devastating instruments has caused offensive action to jump ahead both of defence and of the machinery of diplomacy, and the instruments capable of settling world affairs. He had a remedy with which I heartily agree. The right hon. Gentleman called it the surrender of sovereignty. I do not want to use that word.

Mr. EDEN (Warwick and Leamington) indicated dissent.

Mr. BEVIN: I beg the pardon of the right hon. Gentleman. I do not want to attribute a word to him wrongly. If I have misunderstood it is because it is often suggested by people, when they talk about sovereignty, that what you are asked to do is to surrender your sovereignty. I want to develop my argument that that is not what you do. If I attributed to the right hon. Gentleman what I ought to have attributed to someone else, I am sorry. He said there must be established a rule of law, but law must derive its power and observance from a definite source, and in studying this problem I am driven to ask: Will law be observed, if it is arrived at only by treaty and promises and decisions by governments as at present arranged? In all the years this has broken down so often. I trust it will not break down again but, if it is not to break down again, I think it must lead us still further on. In other words, will the people feel that the law is their law if it is derived and enforced by the adoption of past methods, whether League of Nations, concert of Europe, or anything of that kind? *The illustration was drawn of the constitution of the United Kingdom, which took many years to establish. Where does the power to make law actually rest? It is not even in this House, it is certainly not in the Executive, it is in the votes of the people. They are sovereign authority.*

It may be interesting to call attention to the development of the United States of America. Originally, when the States came together, they met as States with separate governments, but they soon discovered that they had little or no power to enforce their decisions, and it is the enforcement of the decision, the sanction, that is the real difficulty in world law or any law. *They then decided, for the purpose of conducting foreign affairs, taxation, defence, and the regulation of commerce, that they would create a federal body and in that body there would be direct representation of the people, not through the thirteen States, but direct from the people to the Federal Parliament of the country.* So, from the outset, the United States drew its power to make laws directly from the people. That is the growth of the United States to the great State which it is to-day. . . .

We have benefited, at any rate as an Empire, from that decision on two great occasions, because that great country had the foresight to build on the votes of the people. It was the same in Australia, which did not just bring the State governments together but built up the Federal Parliament on the same lines. I used to argue this thing out with the late Lord Lothian and other people for many years, and I am glad to have the opportunity of putting a personal view—not a Cabinet view—because the right hon. Gentleman the Member for Warwick and Leamington raised it yesterday. I think it right to let the country see exactly where the surrender of sovereignty leads us. The fact is, no one ever surrenders sovereignty; they merge it into a greater sovereignty. . . .

The common man, I think, is the great protection against war. The supreme act of government is the horrible duty of deciding matters which affect the life or death of the people. That power rests in this House as far as this country is concerned. I would merge that power into a greater power or a directly elected world assembly in order that the great repositories of destruction and science, on the one hand, may be their property, against the misuse of which it is their duty to protect us, and, on the other hand, that they may determine in the ordinary sense whether a country is acting as an aggressor or not.

I am willing to sit with anybody, of any party, of any nation, to try to devise a franchise or a constitution just as other great countries have done—for a world assembly, as the right hon. Gentleman said, with a limited objective—the objective of peace.

In previous chapters we have seen how the Philadelphia Convention came to see that in order to end the American Revolution the task of preventing war had to be transferred from the thirteen sovereign governments to the people of the United States. The passages italicized in Mr. Bevin's speech show that by some inspiration he had seen that to end the World Revolution the task of preventing war must be transferred from a number of sovereign governments to the people themselves. He was followed by Sir Arthur Salter, the member for Oxford University, whose few words show the profound impression which these speeches made by Mr. Eden and Mr. Bevin had made in the House:

This House and the world will realize that far and away the most important feature of this debate has been what the

Foreign Secretary has just said and what his predecessor said yesterday about the merging of national sovereignty. I profoundly and passionately agree with what they said.

On November 27th Lord Samuel (leader of the Liberal Party) said in the House of Lords:

We have recently read most remarkable speeches by the present and previous Foreign Secretaries, Mr. Bevin and Mr. Eden, advocating that national sovereignty should no longer be absolute and unconditional, responsible to no one. That is a most remarkable development in international policy which, I feel, should be widely welcomed, although I must at once express my agreement with the view put forward by Lord Cranborne—namely, that the federal solution of the election of a universal or a European assembly by a direct vote of all the peoples, while leaving in being all the present Parliaments, would create a situation which would not be likely to conduce to the smooth government of Europe or of the world.

On December 17th Mr. Mackenzie King, Prime Minister of Canada, said to his House of Commons:

As political problems affecting the relations of governments, the solution of the problems presented by atomic energy must be sought in the realm of world politics. The more deeply one ponders the problems with which our world is confronted in the light—'the terrible light,' as Mr. Attlee said—of the implications of the development of atomic energy, the harder it is to see a solution in anything short of some surrender of national sovereignty. With a limited surrender of national sovereignty, there must be instituted some form of world government restricted, at least at the outset, to matters pertaining to the prevention of war, and the maintenance of international security. The United Nations Organization is not a sufficient answer to the problems of peace and security which the world is now seeking. It is a first step, and an all-important step, in the direction of that co-operation between nations which is essential to the survival of civilization. It is not,

however, the only, much less the final, step. The United
Nations Organization is an indispensable medium and
channel and forum through which the peoples of the world
can work out new institutions and arrangements which their
peace and security now require.

He was followed by Mr. Bracken, leader of the
Opposition, who said:

What does it all add up to? If my sixty years tell me
anything, they tell me that humanity will neither be
satisfied nor safe till there is world security against aggressors. Any realist must know that this security will come in
one or other of two ways—the way of war, followed by
slavery to a dominating State, or the way of understanding,
followed by a co-operative world; by force of arms that
will result in a world State, in which one part will be
dominant, or by force of reason in which nations will live
together, each contributing its proper share of the price of
discipline, and each bearing the fruits of the consequent
peace and progress of mankind.

Our path as Canadians is clear. Collective security for
humanity is possible only in international collective agreement. We must pay the price of international collective
agreement. That price is the sacrifice of some degree of
national sovereignty.

Mr. MacInnis, on behalf of the C.C.F., added:

The leader of the Opposition (Mr. Bracken) says we have
come to the stage in world affairs where co-operation is not
only necessary but imperative. Indeed, in my humble
opinion the atomic bomb has brought us to the stage where
world government at the international level is not only a
desirable thing but a necessity. The choice before us is either
world government or world destruction.

Thus, as at Westminster, the leaders of all parties at
Ottawa put the issue above and beyond party divisions.

Why has action been slow to follow these memorable
speeches in the two greatest parliaments of the

Commonwealth? The answer to this question may perhaps be found in what has been said on a previous page of the disposition of permanent officials to keep things as they are. When ministers initiate a new policy it is for their permanent officials to suggest what steps should be taken to carry it into effect. But such is the congestion of business in public departments that permanent officials are constantly at their wits' end to find time for their minister to consider the advice they offer, make decisions, and give instructions. The most pressing matters which are not always the most important tend to find a higher place on the agenda prepared for the minister than matters of greater importance which are not so pressing. In the press of business such matters may in time fade from the minds of the minister and his advisers and be forgotten. Government departments may be compared to refrigerated chests in larders, to which dishes made in the legislature are taken to be kept in cold storage until they can be served. It may happen that dishes of the greatest importance may be put on the highest shelf in the larder, and there be forgotten.

The disposition of civil servants to keep things as they are has a gradual effect on the minds of their chief, of which neither is conscious. Few politicians can work long in Whitehall and not be influenced by the traditional attitude of their highly competent advisers. It is only statesmen who have the personality and initiative of a Lord Grey, a Lloyd George, or a Winston Churchill who can long resist the unconscious assumption of officials that the system they know and work must be maintained.

As Churchill himself remarks in *The Second World War* (p. 374):

> The human mind, except when guided by extraordinary genius, cannot surmount the established conclusions amid which it has been reared.

These were probably the reasons why time passed and nothing was done to translate into action the declarations of statesmen in November, 1945, that nothing less than the merging of national sovereignties in an international sovereignty would avail to stop the drift to a third war. Their speeches, which run counter to all that journalists had written for years, were seldom, if ever, recalled in the Press, and were presently forgotten.

XII

THE MOVEMENT FOR UNITED EUROPE AND THE MARSHALL PLAN

WHEN Mr. Bevin said to the House of Commons that 'the common man is the great protection against war', he had grasped the nature of the World Revolution as the founders of the U.S.A. had done in 1787. Like them he had seen how to end the World Revolution when he added that he was 'willing to sit with anybody, of any party, of any nation, to try to devise a franchise or a constitution, just as other great countries have done—for a world assembly'.

We must now see how the minds of ministers have moved since this great declaration in 1945. As the issues have become the subject of controversy it is best to allow them to speak for themselves. Readers who have followed the movement for Western Union need spend little time on these chapters, though it may be convenient for them to know where to look for the speeches and letters in which political leaders recorded their views. Here and there I have printed words in italics to which I shall have occasion to refer in subsequent chapters. The Table of Contents for Part II will make it easy to find the pages they want.

No further move was made by leaders on either side until on December 30 and 31, 1946, Winston Churchill outlined his policy for uniting Europe in the *Daily Telegraph*. The articles were revised and reprinted by the St. Clement's Press, Portugal Street,

Kingsway, London, W.C.2, under the title *A UNITED EUROPE: One Way to Stop a New War*. In this pamphlet Churchill writes:

Alas, although the resources and vitality of nearly all the European countries are woefully diminished, many of their old hatreds burn on with undying flame. Skeletons with gleaming eyes and poisoned javelins glare at each other across the ashes and rubble-heaps of what was once the august Roman Empire and later a Christian Civilization.

Is there never to be an end? Is there no salvation here below? Are we to sink through gradations of infinite suffering to primordial levels:

> 'A discord. Dragons of the Prime,
> That tare each other in their slime':

or can we avoid our doom?

There is the old story of the Spanish prisoner pining for years in his dungeon and planning to escape. One day he pushes the door. It is open. It has always been open. He walks out free. Something like this opportunity lies before the peoples of Europe to-day. Will they grasp it? Will they be allowed to grasp it? Will they have time?

. . . . .

President Roosevelt declared the Four Freedoms. Of these the chief is 'Freedom from Fear'. This does not mean only the fear of war or fear of the foreign invader. Even more poignant is the fear of the policeman's knock; the intrusion upon the humble dwelling; the breadwinner, the son, the faithful friend, marched away into the night with no redress, no habeas corpus, no trial by jury, no rights of man, no justice from the State.

Such are the conditions which prevail to-day over the greater part of Europe. A horrible retrogression! Back to the Dark Ages, without their chivalry, without their faith.

Yet all this could be ended *at a single stroke*. Two or three hundred millions of people in Europe have only got to

F

wake up one morning and resolve to be happy and free by becoming one family of nations, banded together from the Atlantic to the Black Sea for mutual aid and protection. *One spasm of resolve!* One single gesture! The prison doors clang open. Out walk, or totter, the captives into the sunshine of a joyous world.

I do not at all conceal from the reader that an act of the sublime is required. It is a very simple act, not even a forward bound. Just stand erect, but all together.

．　　　．　　　．　　　．　　　．

Let me use the military modes and terminology with which our sad experience has made us all too familiar. When a great army is formed by a nation or band of allies it has its General Headquarters; but who would pretend, with our experience, that any General Headquarters could deal directly with a mob of brigades and divisions, each headed by their colourful commander, each vaunting the prowess of their own recruiting district or home State, each pleading the particular stresses of their own task and station?

．　　　．　　　．　　　．　　　．

The British nation, lying in the centre of so many healthy and beneficient networks, is not only the heart of the British Empire and Commonwealth of Nations, and an equal partner in the English-speaking world, but it is also a part of Europe and intimately and inseparably mingled with its fortunes. All this interlacement strengthens the foundations and binds together the World Temple.

Let me now set forth tersely what it is we have to do. All the people living in the Continent of Europe have to learn to call themselves Europeans, and act as such so far as they have political power, influence, or freedom. *If we cannot get all countries, we must get all we can*, and there may be many. Once the conception of being European becomes dominant among those concerned, a whole series of positive and practical steps will be open.

．　　　．　　　．　　　．　　　．

The Council of Europe must reach out towards some common form of defence which will preserve order among,

and give mutual security to, its members, and enable Europe
to take an effective part in the decisions of the Supreme
United Nations Organization.

.   .   .   .   .

Mr. Attlee has declared, 'Europe must federate or
perish,' and he does not readily change his opinions.
Prominent names could be cited of men in office and power
in many countries in and out of Europe who hold the same
view. General Smuts, the South Africa soldier-statesman-
philosopher, has proclaimed himself a champion of the
idea. Belgium, Holland, Luxembourg, have already begun
naturally and unostentatiously to put it into practice.

There is much talk of a 'Western bloc'; but that by itself
is too narrow a scheme. Nothing less than Europe and
Europeanism will generate the vital force to survive. It
may well be that everybody cannot join the club at once.
The beginning must be made. *The nucleus must be formed in
relation to the structure as a whole, so that others can join easily*
as soon as they feel inclined or feel able. The ideal is so
commanding that it can afford a gradual realization.

But we are told this conception of a free reviving, re-
generated Europe is anti-Russian, or, to speak more exactly,
anti-Soviet in its character, intention, and effect.

This is not true. The many peoples of Russia who are
comprised in the Union of Soviet Socialist Republics, and
who occupy one-sixth of the land surface of the globe, have
nothing to fear and much to gain from the creation of a
United Europe, more especially as both these groupings
must be comprised within the World Organization and be
faithful to its decisions.

.   .   .   .   .

It seems a shocking thing to say that the atomic bomb
in the guardianship of the United States is the main safe-
guard of humanity against a third world war. In the
twentieth century of the Christian era, with all the march
of science and the spread of knowledge, with all the
hideous experiences through which we have passed, can
it be that only this dread super-sanction stands between
us and further measureless misery and slaughter? Those

of us who were born in the broad liberalism of the nineteenth century recoil from such a mockery of all our dreams, of all our defined conceptions. Nevertheless, I believe the fact is true.

The atomic bomb is the new balancing factor. Of all the deterrents against war now acting upon the minds of men, nothing is comparable to this frightful agency of indiscriminate destruction.

While this supreme weapon rests in the hands of the United States alone, it is probable, though we cannot say it is certain, that a breathing-space will be accorded to the world. We cannot tell how long this breathing space will last. Let us make sure that it is not cast away.

If, in this interval, we can revive the life and unity of Europe and Christendom, and with this new reinforcement build high and commanding the world structure of peace which no one dare challenge, the most awful crisis of history will have passed away and the high road of the future will again become open.

If during the next five years we can build a world structure of irresistible force, and inviolable authority, there are no limits to the blessings which all men may enjoy and share.

For this purpose few things are more important and potentially decisive than that Europe should cease to be a volcano of hatred and strife and should instead become one of those broad upland regions upon which the joy, the peace, and glory of millions may repose.

Churchill was determined that the question of winning the peace should be kept above party lines. In this he was supported by a group of Labour members, including Mr. Mackay, member for Hull (an Australian), and the Rev. Gordon Lang, M.P. He proceeded to organize a committee consisting of people who agreed that a way to prevent war must be found; but on little else. It included members so far apart as Mr. Victor Gollancz, Mr. Oliver Stanley, Lady Violet

Bonham-Carter, Mr. Amery, Professor Gilbert Murray, and myself. I felt that at this stage it was premature to discuss whether the aim which we had in view could be realized by a Western Union on the lines of the American Confederation, the League of Nations, or of the British Commonwealth, or whether the Western Nations could organize a defence too strong for any aggressor to threaten until they had created an organic government for the purpose. This last view was and is my own, and I felt and feel no doubt that when the movement got down to practical details it would come to adopt a plan on the lines worked out in the Leave groups during the war. For the moment I felt that Churchill was right in concentrating public attention on the vital truth that the social, economic, and political problems left by the war were insoluble until, in this atomic age, steps had been taken to prevent the recurrence of war once for all.

In May, 1947, Churchill launched the movement at a meeting in the Albert Hall attended by 8,000 people, under the presidency of the Archbishop of Canterbury, supported by leading members of the Roman Catholic and Free Churches. Churchill's address was received with enthusiasm and arrangements were made to organize an unofficial conference in Europe.

Support for the movement was soon to come from an unexpected quarter. Mr. Marshall, the Secretary of State at Washington, had followed its course with interest. He had seen how difficult it would be for the nations of Europe to unite so long as they were living from hand to mouth, some of them threatened by actual

famine. In a speech at Harvard University on June 5,
1947, he said that:

> There must be some agreement among the countries
> of Europe as to the requirements of the situation and the
> part those countries themselves will take in order to give
> proper effect to whatever action might be undertaken
> by this government. . . .
>
> It would be neither fitting nor efficacious for this
> government to undertake to draw up unilaterally a
> programme designed to place Europe on its feet
> economically. This is the business of the Europeans.

He considered that Europe would need substantial
additional help during the next three or four years,
and thought that

> U.S. assistance should not be doled out as crises
> develop but should provide a cure rather than a mere
> palliative.

On June 13, 1947, Mr. Bevin, in a speech to the
Foreign Press Association in London, said that
although Britain was the centre of a great Empire and
Commonwealth, her destiny was more than ever
linked with that of the rest of Europe. She was a
European nation and must act as such. Referring to
the U.S. offer of aid to Europe, he welcomed it as an
'inspiring lead given to the peoples of Europe' by the
U.S. Secretary of State, and thought that Mr.
Marshall's speech at Harvard would 'rank as one of
the greatest speeches made in world history'. The
government were glad to know that misunderstanding
had been removed by including the U.S.S.R. in the
proposals, thus correcting any impression that there
was anything ideological in this plan, which, Mr.

Bevin said, 'throws a bridge to link East and West'.
He went on:

> *I think the initiative devolves upon us in trying to lead Europe*
> *back to a healthy state.* We in this country are exploring
> urgently and actively how best to respond to this lead
> and must in this work consult France . . . and other
> European nations to see how best to take advantage
> of this great proposal.

At this juncture Mr. Dalton's finance was far from
giving the rest of Europe a lead to a healthier economy.
By the end of the year the British dollar deficit would
be at the rate of about $2\frac{1}{2}$ billion dollars a year. Sir
Stafford Cripps was appointed to the novel post of
Minister of Economic Affairs. His speech to the House
of Commons on October 23, 1947, made public opinion
realize how serious the position was. On November 12th
Mr. Dalton introduced an emergency budget which,
though it represented a considerable step in the right
direction, evoked the criticism that he was more concerned to disculpate himself from responsibility for the
crisis than to take effective measures to meet it. Before
entering the House to introduce it he met a journalist in
the lobby to whom he inadvertently communicated
something of its purport, the upshot of which quickly
appeared in a daily paper. Next day he apologized to
the House for a 'grave indiscretion' and resigned. Sir
Stafford Cripps was appointed Chancellor of the
Exchequer, and inaugurated a severe and courageous
system of finance which quickly won the confidence
of the City and of public opinion.

On November 29, 1947, Mr. Douglas, the U.S.
Ambassador, referring to the Marshall Plan in a speech

at Prestwick, said that it was 'no light undertaking for the United States'. He continued:

There are many who have said my country must engage on this enterprise to preserve its own economic stability. No greater fallacy could be entertained by anyone. Our debts are heavy, our taxes are very high, our position is inflated like a great balloon. We are not a land of inexhaustible treasures. We are suffering very serious shortages, although we have not suffered from the immediate contact of the carnage of war. The United States has drawn upon its resources to an extent which is perhaps not fully comprehended on this side of the Atlantic. If, therefore, we embark on this enterprise, as I hope and believe we shall, we do so only for one moving and compelling reason—to establish stability, decency, and civilized living among the peoples of Europe. Our motives are clean, our ambitions are high, our desires are no less noble than those of the people of any other land.

On December 12, 1947, at a Pilgrims' Dinner, Mr. Marshall spoke on Anglo-American relations. Mr. Bevin, who followed him, said that:

History had decreed that Mr. Marshall's name would be associated with one of the greatest efforts that had ever been made in the establishment of peace—the European recovery programme. When he read that speech at Harvard he must confess that it brought hope. He thought it would go down to history as one of the greatest that had been made in the post-war period. He felt that behind it their guest was really expressing the true generous heart of the American people, with whom it was his good fortune to have been intimately associated for over thirty years. They were not all millionaires in the United States, they were ordinary human folk like themselves. Their basic approach to the future was the same, and they instinctively understood one another.

Returning to the subject in the House of Commons on January 22, 1948, Mr. Bevin said:

'The free nations of Western Europe must now draw closely together. I believe the time is ripe for a consolidation of Western Europe.' As for France, Britain already had and would maintain close contacts, but 'the time had come to find ways and means of developing relations with the Benelux countries'. He went on: 'Yesterday our representatives in Brussels, The Hague, and Luxembourg were instructed to propose such talks in concert with French colleagues. I hope treaties will be signed with the Benelux countries, making, with our treaty with France, an important nucleus in Western Europe. We have then to go beyond the circle of our immediate neighbours . . . and consider the question of associating other historic members of European civilization, including the new Italy, in this great conception. Their eventual participation is, of course, no less important than that of countries with which, if only for geographical reasons, we must deal first. We are thinking now of Western Europe as a unit. The nations of Western Europe have already shown at the Paris Conference dealing with the Marshall Plan their capacity for working together quickly and effectively. That is a good sign for the future.'

Freed from official responsibilities Mr. Dalton now turned his attention to United Europe. In a public speech he said:

The United States of Europe can only fully succeed if all the countries of Western Europe commit themselves . . . to the belief that socialism is the hope of us all.

About this time some Labour members who had made speeches which did not fit in with the official programme of the Socialist Party were warned by the party committee that unless they retracted some words to which they took exception they would be expelled from the party. The committee threatened the Labour members who proposed to attend The Hague Conference that they also would be expelled.

On February 13, 1948, a letter from Dr. J. H. Retinger, Secretary of the International Committee of Movements for European Unity, Paris, to the Chairman of the Labour Party Executive, Mr. Shinwell, hoped that the Executive would reconsider its attitude to the attendance of Labour Party members at the European Conference at The Hague in May. It said that a number of leading continental Socialists had already indicated their intention to attend.

Mr. Churchill said:

> I am sorry that certain elements in the Socialist ranks are trying to make the cause of United Europe a monopoly of the Socialist Party. An important conference of supporters of the European cause is being held at The Hague next May. This event has been welcomed by all parties, other than the Communists, throughout the countries of Western Europe. Alone, the British Labour Party has decided to discourage its members from attending. When I proclaimed this idea at Zürich in September, 1946, I earnestly hoped that it might be at once all-party and above party, but through their petty jealousies and internal divisions, the government are being drawn into the grave and anti-social error of trying to form an exclusive union of the Socialists of Europe.

On the other hand, the executive committee of the Labour Party issued a statement on February 27, 1948, in which the following statement occurs:

> The necessary redirection of national thinking cannot be maintained unless European unity is presented as a

dynamic new ideal. A public declaration of faith in European unity would act as a challenge to the latent idealism of the masses so long nourished on disillusion and despair, and as a continuing spur to international action for the politicians and public servants, whose enthusiasm would otherwise founder under the accumulation of administrative detail.

XIII

THE HAGUE CONFERENCE AND AFTER

THE Hague Conference met on May 7, 1948. There were more than 800 delegates from twenty countries speaking at least twelve different languages. This great gathering had only four days in which to do its work. Proceedings were opened and closed by Churchill. Passages from these two speeches must be quoted:

Great governments have banded themselves together with all their executive power. Sixteen European States are now associated for economic purposes. Five have entered into close economic and military relationship. We hope that this nucleus will in due course be joined by the peoples of Scandinavia, of the Iberian Peninsula, as well as by Italy, who should now resume her full place in the comity of nations. *This is a movement of peoples and not of parties.* There is no room for personal or party jealousies. If there is rivalry of parties, let it be to see which one will distinguish itself most for the common cause. It must be all for all. The movement for European unity, as our draft report declares, must be a positive force, deriving its strength from our common sense of spiritual values. It is a dynamic expression of democratic faith based upon moral conceptions and inspired by a sense of mission. In the centre of our movement stands a charter of human rights, guarded by freedom and sustained by law. It is impossible to separate economics and defence from general political structure. Mutual aid in the economic field and joint military defence must inevitably be accompanied step by step with a parallel policy of closer political unity. It is said with truth that this involves some sacrifice or merger of national sovereignty. But it is also possible to regard it as the gradual sovereignty which can alone protect their diverse and distinctive customs and characteristics and their national traditions, all of which under totalitarian systems, whether Nazi, Fascist, or Communist, would certainly be blotted out.

.   .   .   .   .

How little it is that all the millions of homes in Europe represented here to-day are asking: a fair chance to make a home, to reap the fruits of their toil, to cherish their wives, to bring up their children in a decent manner, and to dwell in peace and safety, without fear or bullying or monstrous burdens and exploitations. The freedom that matters most to-day is freedom from fear. Why should all these hard-working families be harassed, first, as in bygone times, by dynastic and religious quarrels, next by nationalistic ambitions, and finally by ideological fanaticism? Shall so many millions of humble homes in Europe, aye, and much of its enlightenment and culture, sit quaking in dread of the policeman's knock? That is the question which, perhaps, we have the power to answer here. We are here to lay the foundations upon which the statesmen of the Western democracies may stand, and to create an atmosphere favourable to the decisions to which they may be led. It is not for us who do not wield the authority of governments to confront each other or the world with sharply cut formulas or detailed arrangements. There are many different points of view which have to find their focus. We in Britain must move in harmony with our great partners in the Commonwealth, who, I do not doubt, share our aspirations and follow with deep attention our trend of thought. Nevertheless, we must not separate without a positive step forward. We must here and now resolve that in one form or another a European assembly shall be constituted which will enable that voice to make itself continuously heard, and we trust with ever-growing acceptance throughout all the free countries of this continent.

Mr. Churchill absented himself from the Congress between his opening and closing speeches. In his absence the British Delegation was led by Mr. R. W. G. Mackay, M.P., ably supported by Mr. Harold Macmillan, M.P., and Lady Violet Bonham-Carter.

An all-party deputation headed by Churchill and Mackay waited on the Prime Minister and Foreign Secretary at 10 Downing Street on May 17th, and asked the government to take action to give effect to the following resolutions of The Hague Conference.

The Congress

(1) Recognizes that it is the urgent duty of the nations of Europe to create an economic and political union in order to assure security and social progress.

(2) Notes with approval the recent steps which have been taken by some European governments in the direction of economic and political co-operation, but believes that in the present emergency the organizations created are by themselves insufficient to provide any lasting remedy.

Sovereign Rights

(3) *Declares that the time has come when the European nations must transfer and merge some portion of their sovereign rights so as to secure common political and economic action for the integration and proper development of their common resources.*

(4) Considers that any *Union or Federation of Europe* should be designed to protect the security of its constituent peoples, should be free from outside control, and should not be directed against any other nation.

(5) Assigns to a United Europe the immediate task of establishing progressively a democratic social system, the aim of which shall be to free men from all types of slavery and economic insecurity, just as political democracy aims at protecting them against the exercise of arbitrary power.

(6) Affirms that the integration of Germany *in a*

federated Europe alone provides a solution to both the economic and political aspects of the German problem.

(7) Declares that *the Union or Federation* must assist in assuring the economic, political, and cultural advancement of the populations of the overseas territories associated with it, without prejudice to the special ties which now link these territories to European countries.

European Assembly

(8) Demands the convening, as a matter of real urgency, of a European Assembly chosen by the Parliaments of the participating nations, from among their members and others, designed

(*a*) to stimulate and give expression to European public opinion;

(*b*) to advise upon immediate practical measures designed progressively to bring about the necessary economic and political union of Europe;

(*c*) to examine the juridical and constitutional implications arising out of the creation of such *a Union or Federation* and their economic and social consequences;

(*d*) to prepare the necessary plans for the above purposes.

Charter of Human Rights

(9) Considers that the resultant *Union or Federation* should be open to all European nations democratically governed and which undertake to respect a Charter of Human Rights.

(10) Resolves that a Commission should be set up to undertake immediately the double task of drafting such a Charter and of laying down standards to which a State must conform if it is to deserve the name of a democracy.

(11) Declares that in no circumstances shall a State

be entitled to be called a democracy unless it does, in fact as well as in law, guarantee to its citizens liberty of thought, assembly, and expression, as well as the right to form a political opposition.

(12) Requests that this Commission should report within three months on its labours.

Supreme Court

(13) Is convinced that in the interests of human values and human liberty, the Assembly should make proposals for the establishment of a Court of Justice with adequate sanctions for the implementation of this Charter, and to this end any citizen of the associated countries shall have redress before the court, at any time and with the least possible delay, of any violation of his rights as formulated in the Charter.

World Unity

(14) Declares that the creation of a United Europe is an essential element in the creation of a united world.

On June 17, 1948, the following official statement was issued from 10 Downing Street:

The Prime Minister, accompanied by the Secretary of State for Foreign Affairs, received at 10 Downing Street a deputation of British delegates to The Hague Congress, headed by Mr. Winston Churchill.

Mr. Churchill presented to Mr. Attlee copies of three resolutions, political, economic, and cultural, adopted by the Congress, and asked for the sanction and support of His Majesty's Government for these resolutions.

Mr. R. W. G. Mackay, M.P., spoke on the political resolution, Lord Layton on the economic resolution, and Mr. Kenneth Lindsay, M.P., on the cultural resolution.

The deputation also included Mr. Boothby, M.P., Mr. Clement Davies, M.P., Mr. Delargy, M.P., Mr. H. Hynd, M.P., Sir Peter Macdonald, M.P., Mr. Harold

Macmillan, M.P., Sir Arthur Salter, M.P., Mr. C. Shaw-cross, M.P., Major Beddington Behrens, Sir Harold Butler, Lady Violet Bonham-Carter, Mr. Henry Hopkinson, Miss Josephy, Commander S. King-Hall, Lady Rhys-Williams, and Mr. Duncan Sandys.

The Prime Minister stressed the work which was already going forward with the support of His Majesty's Government towards the goal of European unity. He undertook, with the Foreign Secretary, to examine the detailed proposals put in the resolutions and in particular the proposal for the convening of a European Assembly.

On May 31, 1948, Mr. Dalton rejoined the Cabinet as Chancellor of the Duchy of Lancaster.

The following exchange of correspondence between the Prime Minister and Mr. Churchill discloses the attitude of the British Government to the proposals for a European Assembly:

Mr. Churchill

July 27, 1948

My dear Prime Minister

When you were good enough to receive a deputation composed of members of the British delegation to The Hague Congress, it was agreed that further detailed information should be sent to you about the proposal for the convening of a European Assembly.

The paper which I enclose is a tentative scheme prepared by a group of members of the British delegation drawn from all political parties.

The details of the scheme are being worked out by an International Study Committee under the chairmanship of Monsieur Ramadier.

I also enclose a memorandum approved by the International Committee of the Movements for European Unity at its meeting in Paris on July 18th, and a draft resolution to be submitted to each Parliament. The creation of a European Assembly would represent an important practical step in the advance towards a United Europe, and would

G

greatly help to create a sense of solidarity among the European peoples in the face of the increasing dangers which beset them. In this the lead should be taken by Britain.

The encouraging response to the initiative of the Foreign Secretary after the announcement of the Marshall Plan in June, 1947, and, more recently, in the negotiations for the Brussels Treaty are proof, if such is necessary, of the influence of British leadership.

I should therefore be most glad if you would consider this memorandum and its enclosures. We should welcome any criticisms or suggestions you may care to make and should, of course, be glad to come and discuss the matter with you further should you desire it.

Yours sincerely,

WINSTON CHURCHILL.

The Prime Minister

July 30, 1948

My dear Churchill,

On the 27th you wrote me on behalf of an all-party group of the members of the British delegation to The Hague Congress about the proposal for the convening of a European Assembly.

As I told you when we discussed the matter together on July 28th, I am in sympathy with the basic idea behind the movement.

I do not, however, see how the government could support in the United Kingdom Parliament the draft resolution which the International Committee of the Movement for European Unity has suggested should be moved in the Parliaments of the different participating countries.

It seems to me that if an Assembly is to be convened this must, in view of the vital importance of the matter, be done by governments, and not by independent organizations or by Parliaments.

On the other hand, I think that this is not the right time

for governments to take this major initiative, *when their hands are so full already with urgent and difficult problems.*

It seems to me that it would be unfortunate if the chances of action later were to be prejudiced by such a resolution being raised before the government feel able to support it, and I cannot therefore but feel that it would be best that the resolution should not be brought forward at this stage.

But, of course, I see no reason why the independent organizations concerned in the movement should not continue their work of spreading the idea of European Union.

Yours sincerely,

C. R. ATTLEE.

Mr. Churchill

August 21, 1948

My dear Prime Minister,

We were naturally disappointed to receive your letter of July 30th because of its negative character.

I thought it wise to delay its publication until you had returned from your well-deserved holiday, in the hope that events in Europe might win a more favourable reply.

Now that Monsieur Spaak has made his important pronouncement, and that the French Government have not only adopted the policy but officially propose a practical form of action, I venture to hope that His Majesty's Government will find it possible to place themselves more in line with Western European opinions upon an issue which they themselves have done much to promote.

Yours sincerely,

WINSTON S. CHURCHILL.

The Prime Minister

August 21, 1948

My dear Churchill,

I have now received your further letter of August 21st. I note that you now desire that publication should be given to the correspondence which has passed between us about the proposal to convene a European Assembly.

According to Press reports the French Government intend to raise the matter in the first instance with the Brussels Treaty Powers, and in that event the issue will probably be placed on the agenda of the Brussels Treaty Permanent Commission very shortly.

If you consider that in these circumstances the present is a suitable moment at which to publish our correspondence, I should not wish to dissuade you.

I should, however, tell you that when M. Bidault raised the question of a European Assembly at the meeting of the Brussels Treaty Consultative Council at The Hague on July 20th the Foreign Secretary replied that he could not for the time commit himself, and there was general agreement that M. Bidault's statement should be given further consideration by the five governments.

In adopting this line the Foreign Secretary took into account the circumstance that the whole question has an important bearing on Commonwealth relations, and that in consequence the government desire to exchange views with the Commonwealth Prime Ministers in October before expressing any definite view.

But this consideration need not affect the work of independent organizations which, as I suggested in my previous letter, could profitably continue to prepare the grounds for European Union.

Yours sincerely,

C. R. ATTLEE.

On September 15, 1948, speaking in the House of Commons in a Review of Foreign Affairs, Mr. Bevin touched on the matter.

Western Union. There had been a tendency to oversimplify the problem, but he did not want to be forced into action which would stop the process already going on. That was why he was exercising caution. Nations were being brought together for their economic co-operation and their future survival. *The work of devising the economic unity of Europe and later a political association could not be done by some simplified spectacular means, but only by one effort followed by another and dovetailed together in a complete plan.* The countries concerned did not want to be diverted from their efforts by setting up an assembly to draft a constitution. Constitution-making raised great problems: Britain had no written constitution, other countries had; the States of the Commonwealth had no collective constitution. The Commonwealth must be consulted. He considered the right approach to Western Union was that of constant association step by step, by treaty and agreement, by taking on certain things that they would do collectively. When the countries concerned had settled defence, economic co-operation, and political development, then it might be possible to establish some kind of assembly.

Readers who have followed the part played by American politicians from 1783 to 1787 will see how closely it corresponded to the attitude revealed in the foregoing letters and speeches. The reason for this is that the British, like the American, politicians were trying to work an obsolete system which was unworkable. They were both victims of 'the functional approach' to 'a creeping and incipient union'. These attempts to remove the prevailing fear of war by imperceptible steps in either case plunged the public mind into even deeper anxiety. When in 1788 the adoption of the Federal Constitution had transferred the responsibility for preventing war from a number of sovereign governments to the people of the United States, the fear of war at once began to subside. Nothing less than a constitution defining the change which had to be accepted could have removed the fear of war, which had steadily grown, so long as the attempt to remove it was made by imperceptible steps.

The reader may also note that the American politicians who from 1783 to 1787 had followed a futile and humiliating role, had in framing the Federal Constitution and afterwards in giving effect to it emerged as states- men. This remark is of special interest to those who watched the indifferent figure cut by members of the four South African Governments in the years preceding 1909. They, like the American politicians, made a poor show so long as they tried to work an unworkable system. They also, in achieving union and in giving effect to the constitution they had devised, began to emerge as statesmen. We British may draw comfort from these examples and expect that our overworked ministers may appear as statesmen worthy of the greatest opportunity ever offered to rulers, when once they realize that the functional approach to a creeping and incipient union has merely increased and deepened the fear of war in the public mind.

The letters exchanged between Mr. Attlee and Mr. Churchill aroused searchings of heart in Washington. Mr. Walter Lippmann, who has been described as America's unofficial Foreign Secretary, and is known to reflect the views of the State Department, published a syndicated article from which the following extracts are made:

In the not distant future the attitude of the British Labour Government toward European unity is likely to come in for serious discussion on both sides of the Atlantic.

For without the active leadership of the British Govern- ment the economic co-operation envisaged in the Marshall Plan cannot develop.

· · · · ·

The Western Union, which was formed at Brussels, will remain an impotent military alliance unable to evolve into a political system which would restore the power and influence of the European community.

First Essential

American dollars and American guarantees of military support are essential to the security and revival of Europe. But unless Europe is united little can be accomplished.

Not even Western Europe can, or will, begin to unite unless Britain, the strongest of the European nations, is affirmatively and actively the leader in the movement towards European unity.

But Mr. Attlee and Mr. Bevin and Sir Stafford Cripps are making it very plain that the Labour Government will not now take the leaderships, that it is participating reluctantly, without faith or conviction, and only as much as it finds it necessary or expedient in order to placate Mr. Churchill and France and the United States.

Yet Mr. Attlee has said that Europe must federate or perish.

Why, then, is the Attlee Government now so unwilling to lead, so reluctant to follow the movement toward European unity?

Why is the Socialist Government in the United Kingdom, allegedly the most progressive in the world, the most inclined to drag its feet when it is asked to promote that most progressive of all international ideals, the unity of Europe?

Why is it that in the present crisis of Western civilization this British Socialist Government is so much more jealously concerned with the exclusive sovereignty of the United Kingdom than is that tremendous patriot Mr. Winston Churchill, the proven defender of British institutions and of the British Commonwealth and Empire?

System-bound

The reason, I think, is that the Socialist experiment in the United Kingdom has become such a complicated structure of government plans and government controls that it cannot be maintained and managed except by an ever-increasing exercise of the sovereign power of the Central Government.

Having assumed vast and intricate powers over exports, imports, investments, management, expenditure, consumption, work, and the currency, the Socialist Government shrinks from any proposal which would require it to relinquish or even to share any of its sovereign power.

When in Power

Defence of socialism in Great Britain is making, indeed has made, the Labour Government more and more nationalist in its foreign policy.

The original idealism of the Western democratic Socialists was always 'internationalist'. But when Socialists come into power, and if they continue to be Socialists, then socialism becomes inexorably a nationalist socialism.

They cannot help it. When a government undertakes to plan and direct the economic life of a nation it is drawing very heavily on the sovereign power of the national State.

Inevitably it will cling jealously to that sovereign power: since it cannot let private interests at home, it certainly cannot let foreign governments abroad interfere with its planning and its direction of the national economy.

These considerations will help to explain why a non-Socialist like Mr. Churchill, why non-Socialist Governments in France and Italy, why the non-Socialist United States, why the very non-Socialist Mr. Dewey, Mr. Dulles, Mr. Vandenberg, Mr. Lodge, Mr. Hoffmann are now more strongly in favour of European political union than are Mr. Attlee, Mr. Bevin, and Sir Stafford Cripps.

Therefore, it is said the British Labour Government cannot now unite with France and Italy since they are moving away from socialism.

Next winter, when Congress will have to review the recovery programme, this problem may become sharply defined.

To this American view is appended for subsequent reference the momentous address by General Omar N. Bradley, Chief of Staff, United States Army, before the Armistice Day luncheon, Boston Chamber of Commerce, Boston, Massachusetts, at 1.30 p.m. est., on Wednesday, November 10, 1948.

To-morrow is our day of conscience.

For although it is a monument to victory, it is also a symbol of failure. Just as it honours the dead, so must it humble the living.

Armistice Day is a constant reminder that we won a war and lost a peace.

It is both a tribute and an indictment. A tribute to the men who died that their neighbours might live without fear of aggression. An indictment of those who lived and forfeited their chance for peace.

Therefore, while Armistice Day is a day for pride, it is for pride in the achievements of others—humility in our own.

Neither remorse nor logic can hide the fact that our armistice ended in failure. Not until the armistice myth exploded in the blast of a Stuka bomb did we learn that the winning of wars does not in itself make peace. And not until Pearl Harbour did we learn that non-involvement in peace means certain involvement in war.

We paid grievously for those faults of the past in deaths, disaster, and dollars.

It was a penalty we knowingly chose to risk. We made the choice when we defaulted on our task in creating and safeguarding a peace.

Now new weapons have made the risk of war a suicidal hazard. Any nation which does not exert its vigour, wealth, and armed strength in the avoidance of conflict before it strikes, shall endanger its survival. It is no longer possible to shield ourselves with arms alone against the ordeal of attack, For modern war visits destruction on the victor and the vanquished alike. Our only complete assurance of surviving World War III is to halt it before it starts.

For that reason we clearly have no choice but to face the challenge of these strained times. To ignore the danger of aggression is simply to invite it. It must never again be said of the American people: Once more we won a war; once more we lost a peace. If we do we shall doom our children to a struggle that will take their lives.

Armed forces can wage wars but they cannot make peace. For there is a wide chasm between war and peace— a chasm that can only be bridged by good will, discussion, compromise, and agreement. In 1945, while still bleeding from the wounds of aggression, the nations of this world met in San Francisco to build that span from war to peace. For three years—first hopefully, then guardedly, now fearfully—free nations have laboured to complete that bridge. Yet again and again they have been obstructed by a nation whose ambitions thrive best on tension, whose leaders are scornful of peace except on their own impossible terms.

The unity with which we started that structure has been riddled by fear and suspicion. In place of agreement we are wrangling dangerously over the body of that very nation whose aggression had caused us to seek each other as allies and friends.

Only three years after our soldiers first clasped hands over the Elbe, this great wartime ally has spurned friendship with recrimination, it has clenched its fists and skulked in conspiracy behind its secretive borders.

As a result to-day we are neither at peace nor war. Instead we are engaged in this contest of tension, seeking agreement with those who disdain it, rearming, and struggling for peace.

Time can be for or against us.

It can be for us if diligence in our search for agreement equals the vigilance with which we prepare for a storm.

It can be against us if disillusionment weakens our faith in discussion—or if our vigilance corrodes while we wait.

Disillusionment is always the enemy of peace. And to-day—as after World War I—disillusionment can come from expecting too much, too easily, too soon. In our impatience we must never forget that fundamental differences have divided this world; they allow no swift, no cheap, no easy solutions.

While as a prudent people we must prepare ourselves to encounter what we may be unable to prevent, we nevertheless must never surrender ourselves to the certainty of that encounter.

For if we say there is no good in arguing with what must inevitably come, then we shall be left with no choice but to create a garrison state and empty our wealth into arms. The burden of long-term total preparedness for some indefinite but inevitable war could not help but crush the freedom we prize. It would leave the American people soft victims for bloodless aggression.

Both the East and the West to-day deprecate war. Yet because of its threatening gestures, its espousal of chaos, its secretive tactics, and its habits of force—one nation has caused the rest of the world to fear that it might recklessly resort to force rather than be blocked in its greater ambitions.

The American people have said both in their aid to Greece and in the reconstruction of Europe that any threat to freedom is a threat to our own lives. For we know that unless free peoples stand boldly and united against the forces of aggression, they may fall wretchedly, one by one, into the web of oppression.

It is fear of the brutal unprincipled use of force by reckless nations that might ignore the vast reserves of our defensive strength that has caused the American people to enlarge their air, naval, and ground arms.

Reluctant as we are to muster this costly strength, we must leave no chance for miscalculation in the mind of any aggressor.

Because in the United States it is the people who are

sovereign, the government is theirs to speak their voice and to voice their will, truthfully and without distortion.

We, the American people, can stand cleanly before the entire world and say plainly to any State:

'This government will not assail you.

'You can have no conflict without being yourselves the aggressor.'

Since the origin of the American people, their chief trait has been the hatred of war. And yet these American people are ready to take up their arms against aggression and destroy if need be by their might any nation which would violate the peace of the world.

There can be no compromise with aggression anywhere in the world. For aggression multiplies—in rapid succession—disregard for the rights of man. Freedom when threatened anywhere is at once threatened everywhere.

No more convincing an avowal of their peaceful intentions could have been made by the American people than by their offer to submit to United Nations the secret of the atom bomb. Our willingness to surrender this trump advantage that atomic energy might be used for the peaceful welfare of mankind splintered the lies of those word-warmakers that our atom had been teamed with the dollar for imperialistic gain.

Yet because we asked adequate guarantees and freedom of world-wide inspection by the community of nations itself, our offer was declined and the atom has been recruited into this present contest of nerves. To those people who contend that secrecy and medieval sovereignty are more precious than a system of atomic control, I can only reply that it is a cheap price to pay for peace.

The atom bomb is far more than a military weapon. It may—as Bernard Baruch once said—contain the choice between the quick and the dead. We dare not forget that the advantage in atomic warfare lies with aggression and surprise. If we become engaged in an atom bomb race, we may simply lull ourselves to sleep behind an atomic stockpile. The way to win an atomic war is to make certain it never starts.

With the monstrous weapons man already has, humanity is in danger of being trapped in this world by its moral adolescents. Our knowledge of science has clearly outstripped our capacity to control it. We have too many men of science; too few men of God. We have grasped the mystery of the atom and rejected the Sermon on the Mount. Man is stumbling blindly through a spiritual darkness while toying with the precarious secrets of life and death. The world has achieved brilliance without wisdom, power without conscience. Ours is a world of nuclear giants and ethical infants. We know more about war than we know about peace, more about killing than we know about living.

This is our twentieth century's claim to distinction and to progress.

In our concentration on the tactics of strength and resourcefulness which have been used in the contest for blockaded Berlin, we must not forget that we are also engaged in a long-range conflict of ideas. Democracy can withstand ideological attacks if democracy will provide earnestly and liberally for the welfare of its people. To defend democracy against attack, men must value freedom. And to value freedom they must benefit by it in happier and more secure lives for their wives and their children.

Throughout this period of tension in which we live, the American people must demonstrate conclusively to all other peoples of the world that democracy not only guarantees man's human freedom, but that it guarantees his economic dignity and progress as well. To practise freedom and make it work, we must cherish the individual, we must provide him the opportunities for reward and impress upon him the responsibilities a free man bears to the society in which he lives.

The American people cannot abdicate in this present struggle and leave the problem to their armed forces. For this is not a test of combat strength but a contest of resolution. It is dependent less upon military strength and more upon human strength, faith, and fortitude among such citizens as you. If we are to combat communism, we cannot oppose it with anti-communism. We cannot fight something with nothing. More than ever before, we must alert our people—and people throughout the world—to the meaning of their freedom and stimulate in each of them an awareness of their own, their personal share in this struggle.

Good citizenship is the start of a working democracy. And good citizenship begins at home, in the ability of every American to provide a happy and wholesome life for his family. From such simple beginnings do we create better communities, better States, a better nation—and eventually, we hope, a better world.

To you in the greater community of New England much has been given in the heritage that began with Concord, and in the truths that have been left for you by your Lowells, your Emersons, your Holmes.

Out of so fortunate a spiritual start in the meaning and significance of freedom, you have constructed an industrial machine with which to nourish great faith in it.

If we will only believe in democracy, use it, and practise its precepts in the factory as well as the voting booth, we shall so strengthen ourselves that nothing can prevail against us—or against those who stand with us in like good faith.

XIV

SPEECHES BY CHURCHILL, GOLLANCZ, AND SALISBURY

IN November, 1948, speeches were made which showed the respective positions of Churchill, Gollancz, and of Lord Salisbury.

On November 17th the United Europe Exhibition was opened by Winston Churchill, who referred to the division of opinion revealed in the previous chapters as follows:

There has recently been much public discussion about the constitutional form which a United Europe should take. On this question opinion is very divided. There are those who advocate the immediate creation of a European customs union and a complete political federation. There are others who consider that close consultation between governments is the most that can be hoped for, and who regard any form of constitutional or organic union as utterly impracticable.

Each of these views is partly right and partly wrong. To imagine that Europe to-day is ripe for either a political federation or a customs union would be wholly unrealistic. But who can say what may not be possible to-morrow? Anyone who two years ago had had the audacity to predict that by now Western Europe would have a joint economic planning organization and a combined military staff, would have been taken seriously by nobody. Under the mounting pressure of danger and necessity, conceptions which may seem impracticable to-day may quite possibly be thought obvious and inevitable in a few years' time.

My advice is not to attempt at this stage to define too precisely the exact constitutional form which will ultimately emerge. We would do better to concentrate our united efforts on immediately practicable steps.

Let us not underrate the progress which has already been made in the field of inter-governmental co-operation during the last twelve months. Through the medium of the Marshall Plan and the Brussels Pact, changes amounting to nothing less than a revolution in our international relationships, have been brought about. This machinery for joint consultation and planning must be maintained and strengthened and its scope expanded.

But what is good for governments is also good for peoples. They, too, through their representatives, must meet together to consult one another upon these great issues which so intimately affect the lives of every European family. Precisely for this purpose The Hague Congress last May recommended the immediate creation of a consultative European Assembly. This proposal has been officially adopted by the French and Belgian Governments, which have rightfully emphasized that the Assembly must be consultative in character and can have no legislative or constitution-making powers.

It may, of course, be argued that a purely deliberative Assembly would develop into an irresponsible talking-shop, that it would be better to leave the work of European unification to be achieved through inter-governmental negotiations. That is not true. The assembly will perform an essential task and one which cannot be performed by governments; the task of creating a European public opinion and sense of solidarity among the peoples of Europe.

The creation of a deliberative European Assembly naturally involves no transfer of sovereignty and raises no constitutional problems whatsoever. If the British Government decides to give its support to this proposal which has been put forward by the governments of France and Belgium, the European Assembly will assuredly become an accomplished reality. It is therefore to be hoped that our government, which has publicly proclaimed its belief in the principle of European unity, will not hesitate.

Churchill was followed by Victor Gollancz, who said:

Mr. Churchill is the most splendid and significant of— shall I say, of course Englishmen, but also of non-Socialists. I, in the same formula, am the most miserable and insignificant of Socialists. I can only think that it was someone who took a delight in the intellectual beauty of that contrast that suggested I should speak this afternoon. But as that decision has been taken I think it right that I should speak quite definitely and overtly as a Socialist and it's as a Socialist that I want to make, extremely briefly, the three points I am about to make. The first note I want to strike is the note of urgency. This United Europe Movement is not just a good idea that it may be desirable to bring into being in five years' time or ten years' time or fifty years' time. European unity is a matter the urgency of which cannot possibly be exaggerated, because unless a European union of a genuine sort is brought into being in, I would say, not merely a space of a few years, but even a space of a few months, events may very rapidly overtake us. I have myself been obsessed with the idea ever since 1933. I was obsessed month after month by the terrible feeling that events were overtaking us and that everything that we might do would be too late. I have exactly the same feeling now, and I think, therefore, we have to envisage this enterprise not merely as a thing good in itself, but a thing which depends on the rapidity with which it is carried out.

Now the second note that I want to strike is the note of opportunity. There are many propositions that are extremely urgent that cannot be carried out because the opportunity does not arise, because public opinion is not ready for it. For instance, again speaking as an unregenerate Socialist, I should say that socialism was an extremely urgent matter in the thirties, but it could not possibly be carried out because the electorate were at that time plunged in abysmal ignorance. Well, now, what have we in the case of this United Europe Movement? We have an exactly opposite situation. I have been a great deal in the last few years in the three countries—in France, in

H

Germany, and in the United States—and, progressively in all those countries, there is a tremendous feeling that European unity is what everybody wants. It's the most extraordinary thing, wherever you go, as I say, whether it's in Germany or in America, you get this feeling of a tremendous wave of popular opinion behind this movement, and of course its very largely due to the magic of Mr. Churchill's advocacy, and it's one of the things to which, above all, we owe him such gratitude in this movement.

Now, if we have this urgency and this opportunity, for heaven's sake let us wed the opportunity to the need while there is time. I remember, before I started my own publishing business, I was a member of a firm of whom the head used to say, 'You can lose money on a gold mine if you take long enough over it'. That is profoundly true of this European Movement. If we take long enough over it, there will be no Europe left to reorganize.

Now the third point I want to make is the point that has to do with priority. I have already said that I am a Socialist and I have always made it perfectly clear in this movement that what I passionately want to see is a United Socialist States of Europe and that I do not myself believe that the union can be achieved in the fullest sense unless it be a socialist union. I have said that repeatedly, and I would like to say that Mr. Churchill has never made the smallest attempt to modify the strength with which I have put that point of view forward. There has always been complete freedom within our movement, subject to one's belief in the movement, to say exactly what one likes. I say, then, that I believe immensely and passionately in a Socialist State of Europe, but there is a priority greater in my mind than even the priority of the Socialist State of Europe, and that is the priority of United Europe itself. That is the first priority because unless we get a United Europe we shall have no Europe in which we can build the socialism I desire to see. That being so, I do regard as the height of folly any tendency on the part of members of any party, including my own, to say they will not take part in this movement unless the entire movement can be run in accordance with their own political convictions. This is a fatal point of view with which I personally will have nothing whatever to do and which I will oppose inside my own party. It has always seemed to me extremely foolish to talk of European union and to say it must at once be a Socialist Europe when we know that the governments we have to work with at the present time and with whom we can bring this European union into being are, for the most part, not Socialist Governments at all. I therefore do regard this question of priority as a very important one. Let us unite on the question of United Europe as a matter of the very first urgency, advocating within our movement and advocating in conferences abroad the particular kind of union we ourselves want.

On November 24, 1948, the Marquess of Salisbury told the House of Lords:

There was only one thing that mattered to-day and that was national defence and the prevention of war. We must do everything that was necessary at whatever sacrifice to achieve that result. If another war came all England would be swept away by the welter of confusion that would ensue. Let the government tell the people the truth and ask for their co-operation and they would not be disappointed. (*The Times*, November 25, 1948.)

XV

STEPS IN THE MOVEMENT FOR WESTERN UNION

DELEGATES of the five Brussels Treaty Powers were to meet in Paris in November. The French delegation was led by M. Herriot and included two other former Prime Ministers, M. Reynaud and M. Blum. The British delegation was led by Mr. Dalton. Its other members were Lord Inverchapel, Sir Edward Bridges, Professor Wade, and Mr. Gill, Chairman of the Co-operative Society. Holland sent Mr. Albards, Councillor of State, Dr. Slot a journalist, and Mr. Kerstens, Chairman of the European Movement, Dutch Council. M. Loesch and M. Resquin represented Luxembourg. The Belgian delegation of M. Buzet, M. De Schrijver, and Professor De Housse was led by M. Spaak the Prime Minister. At that moment his government resigned, but he formed another in time for the Paris Committee to meet on November 26th.

The French and Belgian Governments proposed the election by Parliaments of a European consultative assembly. The British Government proposed a European Council of Ministers appointed by governments.

On December 9th Mr. Bevin, reviewing the policy of His Majesty's Government in the House of Commons, said that the Brussels Powers' determination to defend themselves had been reflected in the establishment of a common defence policy with a common command and a permanent organization to deal with equipment and supply.

Mr. Bevin went on:

I make this prophecy; I am quite certain that before many years have passed it will be found—it will not be done by me, but it will be found—that the defence ministers and the finance ministers of the Western world particularly will be sitting down together discussing a common budget and a common task and a common method of defence in order that they may protect themselves and carry it upon the resources of their own countries. It will be inevitable and it will come.

We are in favour of extending the principle of the Western system in Europe. With this end in view the government proposed at the meeting in Paris last October of the consultative council of the Brussels Treaty that there should be a European Council of Ministers meeting at regular intervals to provide a forum for dealing with the problems that are common to them. The French and Belgian Governments proposed the creation of a European Assembly without executive power. It is necessary, I think, at this point to remind the House of the decision which the consultative council took.

The Committee is now at work. It is really a working party. I have seen criticisms of the personnel we appointed on it, but they are people with experience. It is led by my right hon. Friend the Chancellor of the Duchy of Lancaster, and I know that they are all working very hard. (Interruption.) Let me say this. If the Prime Minister of this country takes a member into his Cabinet he takes him into his Cabinet to do the jobs that that Cabinet needs to do.

I have served in one previous government. I never questioned the man who was to be working alongside me in that government, and I am not going to question the Prime Minister's decision in this government. If a man is working alongside me I am going to work along with him.

There are two considerations to bear in mind. The Brussels Pact deals with defence. The Western Union may have to deal with problems which will not involve defence. Certain countries may come into the Western Union but not come into the defence pact. Therefore, at a suitable stage, we must consult Scandinavia, we must consult Italy and these other Powers around us and see what is necessary— (Hon. Members: 'Spain?') Spain would be easy if only Franco would disappear—if the thing is to be worked out constructively. I am against using any promises or façades to lead people to believe that they have something which, when the test comes, does not work. I will not comment on another international institution about the effectiveness of which all of us at the moment are gravely concerned. One other point (Interruption)—Well, the United Nations is giving us grave concern as to whether it is going to face the serious problems involved.

There is one other thing I must mention in this connection. We have had a Commonwealth Conference and have entered into a great deal of consultation about co-operation, defence, and all kinds of measures. We cannot recklessly assume undertakings in connection with Europe without carrying with us the Commonwealth in complete understanding. Because in the end it is the combination of Western Union with those great countries of the Commonwealth which, as I said in a previous speech, is bound to be the stabilizing influence in the world.

* * * * *

I am reminded that the communiqué we issued contained a reference to this matter, and, so far as I know, on the question of Western Union there was complete understanding, but not as to a European Assembly. I must not commit them to that, or the form it would take. But as regards the main principle—namely, co-operation with Western Union—there was complete understanding. That is what I meant.

* * * * *

Mr. Schuman declared that the security of Europe cannot be the responsibility of one country, however powerful. Europe must be a common achievement in which Germany must find a place, first of all economically and then politically. The stage has not been reached when we can do the things we want to do politically, but we can do an enormous lot in the political field. Discussions have gone on in the Italian Parliament during which the Prime Minister and the Foreign Minister both made statements in which they identified Italy with the cause of Western democracy. We welcomed these statements and we look forward to an early association of Italy in this work.

I do not think anyone can deny that there is a growing spirit of European solidarity. It is reflected in the great interest in the discussions that are going on. We welcome that. The only thing I would say is that we may have to build a little slower, for we have to build methodically. We must refuse to be stampeded into unpractical if attractive expedients, but we shall give way to none in our desire to achieve the ultimate objective. I venture to suggest that His Majesty's Government have during the last year done more than anyone to promote European collaboration and effort in the economic field, and greater understanding in the political field. At the same time—and this is so vital— we have carried with us other people both in the Commonwealth and in other countries, and this, as the votes in the U.N. at Paris have shown recently, is beginning to create a situation in which not only is the outlook of the Western democracies becoming predominant but also their solidarity is growing and they are on the way towards attaining their security and their final triumph.

. . . . .

Mr. EDEN (Warwick and Leamington): I do not want to argue now the merits of the various proposals and take up the time of the House, but I must point out that the appointment of the right hon. Gentleman the Chancellor of the Duchy caused surprise, and indeed dismay, among many people, not only on these benches but among other parties also. I will say frankly that I believe that if we are to realize a Western Union at all we have to understand that there will be in each country at the same time governments from democratic parties and of the Right, and governments of a wide variety of political opinion. That is inevitable. Sometimes there will be a radical majority, sometimes a Socialist majority, and sometimes a Conservative majority. Our determination must be that we want this organization to work for the attainment of Western Union, irrespective of the domestic political views in one country or another. The Foreign Secretary has never said anything that has differed from that.

The right hon. Gentleman the Chancellor of the Duchy has. He has said exactly the opposite. At his party conference last year he told us quite clearly that the idea of a United States of Europe could only be successful on a Socialist basis. I have his words. He said:

'If this United States of Europe is indeed to succeed and is to benefit its peoples, it can only fully succeed if all the countries of Western Europe commit themselves, as our electors in 1945 committed themselves, to the belief that socialism is the hope of us all.'

Mr. GALLACHER: Hear, hear.

Mr. EDEN: Well, one hon. Member agrees with the right hon. Gentleman on the Front Bench. I must confess that to me that statement seems to be complete nonsense. It must seem complete nonsense to the very large non-Socialist majorities in all the countries of Western Europe at the present time, including Great Britain. . . .

What I want the hon. Gentleman and the House to face is that, if one really thinks that one can only get it on the basis of socialism, one is not going to get Western Union at all. It is no use going to the other countries and saying, 'We will make Western Union with you if you are all Socialists'. The next thing is that, at the next General Election, the Socialists are out, and where then are these countries? They will have to start all over again.

The CHANCELLOR OF THE DUCHY OF LANCASTER (Mr. DALTON): Perhaps I also might be allowed to interrupt the right hon. Gentleman. I hope, if Mr. Speaker so wills, that I may have a chance of saying something to-morrow. But may I ask the right hon. Gentleman if any further quotations are to be discovered from my remarks, because this is an accurate but highly selective quotation?

Mr. EDEN: Here is another one which says:

'In my opinion, speaking also for my colleagues on the Executive, we are quite confident that the success of any scheme for a United States of Europe, however defined, for the peoples composing the aggregate population of Western Europe, is going to depend upon the success of those democratic Socialist parties in each of those countries taken separately, and in all those countries taken together.'

It seems to me to amount to much the same as the previous quotation. If I have misrepresented the right hon. Gentleman I hope he will tell me. I beg the House to face the fact that if we are going to get Western Union in this generation—united Western Union in this generation—we shall not get it on the basis of one particular party, or one particular dogma.

Mr. ZILLIACUS (Gateshead): . . . We should also insist on the introduction of sufficient elements of socialism into the political economies of Western Europe as a condition for our joining up with them, otherwise our own planned economy will suffer.

Mr. CHURCHILL (Woodford): . . . This brings me naturally to what is called Western Union, in respect of which the greatest credit will rest upon the right hon. Gentleman and the Cabinet of which he is the Foreign Secretary. It brings me not only to Western Union but to the wider United Europe Movement which has been its herald and will always be its friend, helper, and servitor. *The swiftest means of bringing Germany back into Western Europe—preferably, as I have said, on a basis of States*—may well be found in this European movement in the first instance. It may well be. And when one considers countries like Belgium, Holland, Luxembourg, and so on, many German States are much larger and more powerful, much more numerous in population than these, and I cannot see why there should not be a continuous confluence of ideas and goodwill between them all.

Here, when we come to the European movement, I must part company with the government and the Foreign Secretary. The attitude of the Socialist Party under their guidance has hitherto been far from creditable and below the level of these important world and human events. Petty personal jealousies and party rancour have marred their actions and falsified their principles. We all remember how the government and their party organization tried to wreck The Hague Conference in May, and how they failed. Last week, at Question Time, I complained about the composition of the delegation which the government had sent to the Conference on European Unity which is still meeting in Paris. The Government seem to be absolutely and obstinately determined to keep this movement towards the unity of so many people who are divided by such grievous feuds as a party preserve for the Socialists.

My right hon. Friend the Member for Warwick and Leamington yesterday referred to this in scathing terms, and dwelt upon the folly and conceit of such an idea. The movements toward European unity, as he said, cannot be a monopoly of any party; least of all should it at this moment become the monopoly of a party which, in many parts of Europe, has shown in a most lamentable fashion its inherent weakness when exposed to the serious attacks of communism. The movement towards European unity can only achieve success through the reconciliation and goodwill of whole peoples, irrespective of their internal political or party bias, divisions, or labels.

We are not seeking in the European movement—and I speak as one of the Presidents; I share that honour with M. Blum and with the Prime Minister of Italy and the Prime Minister of Belgium, M. Spaak—to usurp the functions of government. I have tried to make this plain again and again to the heads of the government. We ask for a European Assembly without executive power. We hope that sentiment and culture, the forgetting of old feuds, the lowering and melting down of barriers of all kinds between countries, the growing sense of being 'a good European'—we hope that all these will be the final, eventual,

and irresistible solvents of the difficulties which now con-
demn Europe to misery. The structure of constitutions, the
settlement of economic problems, the military aspects—
these belong to governments. We do not trespass upon their
sphere. But I am sure there is no government whole-
heartedly loyal to the idea of European unity which would
not be invigorated and sustained by the creation of a
European Assembly such as we asked for at The Hague,
and such as is now proclaimed and asked for by three, if
not four, out of the five Powers which now comprise the
Western Union.

For this reason the composition of the British delegation
to the Conference which is now proceeding came as a shock.
It came as a shock not only to a great body of opinion in
both parties in this Island, but to all those powerful elements
of European opinion to which we understood so many
British Labour men hoped to make their special appeal.
Nothing could have been more astonishing than the
appointment of the Chancellor of the Duchy of Lancaster
as the leader of the delegation after the line he had taken
and the speeches, quoted yesterday by my right hon.
Friend the Member for Warwick and Leamington, which
he had delivered recently. He has been the great opponent
of the idea of this European movement—

The CHANCELLOR OF THE DUCHY OF LANCASTER (Mr.
DALTON) indicated dissent.

Mr. CHURCHILL: —except on Socialist Party lines. In
commenting on this appointment by the Prime Minister
the right hon. Gentleman the Foreign Secretary used some
guarded language, indicating how it was his duty to take
anyone who was put alongside him.

The SECRETARY OF STATE FOR FOREIGN AFFAIRS (Mr.
ERNEST BEVIN): I hope I did not convey to the right hon.
Gentleman that I was not a party to the appointment of my
right hon. Friend, because I have absolute confidence in
him in doing the job.

Mr. CHURCHILL: The right hon. Gentleman naturally
has to express his confidence, but he should read carefully
what he said, because a more chilling welcome to a comrade

and colleague I have rarely heard expressed. I say that the appointment of the right hon. Gentleman after the speeches he has made—unexplained, unretracted in any way—wore the aspect of nothing less than to resolve to sabotage the conception—

Mr. DALTON indicated dissent.

Mr. CHURCHILL: —of European unity except on a Socialist Party basis. I have also criticized on different grounds the appointment of Sir Edward Bridges. There is no man I respect more, but he is the head of the Civil Service and I do not think the Prime Minister should have brought him into this sphere, which is necessarily controversial. The right hon. Gentleman said at Question Time that it was quite normal for governments to employ civil servants when they have government representatives going to conferences. He said how my right hon. Friend, the late Foreign Secretary, had often—invariably, in fact—taken his civil servants and advisers from the Foreign Office with him. The right hon. Gentleman completely misses the point. It is an absurd argument to use in this connection. Of course civil servants may go to conferences to assist ministers, but to take the head of the Civil Service and make him a delegate to meet the former Prime Ministers of other countries, and so forth, in a matter about which opinions differ in parties and between parties, is an abuse for which there is only one precedent that I know of and that is not a good one.

. . . . .

We do not know what line the Chancellor of the Duchy is going to take. He is to make a speech and we shall be glad to hear it. Far be it from me to set aside any hopes of his reform or of a modification in the attitude of the government towards the consultative and deliberative European Assembly. I await his reply. I am willing to judge his attitude by it. It is never too late to mend, or, if I may, on account of his ecclesiastical upbringing, use another similitude: 'Betwixt the stirrup and the ground he mercy sought, and mercy found.'

If the right hon. Gentleman feels able to make a declaration to-day in the sense in which I have spoken he will improve the reputation of the government among the Western Allies and in the United States. If he will not, if he only goes over the old ground of the speeches he delivered to the T.U.C. and at other party meetings, the general condemnation of the government's attitude, and of the Foreign Secretary's attitude—because it is felt that he has played a leading part in this attempt to hamper and break down the unofficial and private efforts that have been made to build up this public opinion in favour of a United Europe—will be extended and emphasized and the Chancellor of the Duchy himself will have entered another large sphere of activity only to distract, confuse, and vitiate it. I hope, however, that we shall hear something encouraging from him to-day, not only with regard to the salvation of a single human being, but about the larger issues which concern us in Europe.

The CHANCELLOR OF THE DUCHY OF LANCASTER (Mr. DALTON):

. . . We are conducting very friendly and constructive discussions in Paris. At the first meeting, at my proposal, M. Herriot, that very distinguished French man of State, was appointed President. It was universally approved that he should occupy that position. We have been studying in our discussions in Paris the practical and detailed aspects of the problem, and various proposals that have been made from various quarters. There is a British proposal for the creation of a Council of Europe. There is a French proposal for the creation of a Consultative Assembly. There are other intermediate proposals, other suggestions made by private organizations with some of which the right hon. Gentleman is connected.

I have made it quite clear that so far as the British delegation is concerned—and the other delegations have agreed with us—we are happy to hear witnesses, to listen to statements of opinion, and to receive memoranda from private bodies which have views on this matter. Only yesterday Mr. Duncan Sandys and various of his colleagues were giving evidence. I was very sorry that I could not

be there, but I had to be here. The day before my hon.
Friend the Member for North-West Hull (Mr. Mackay),
who has played a great part in these affairs, and some of his
colleagues were giving evidence. I mention these facts
merely in order to illustrate our procedure. We are
willing to receive evidence from responsible quarters when
it is offered.

But, as my right hon. Friend the Foreign Secretary
explained yesterday, we are a fact-finding body. We are,
if one cares to use the term, a working party. I would like
to quote the words which the Foreign Secretary used
yesterday about this matter. He quoted the terms of
reference of the committee, about which he said there had
been some misunderstanding. The terms of reference were:

'To consider and report to governments on the steps
to be taken towards securing a greater measure of unity
between European countries . . .'

and he went on to quote in detail. Then he said:

'This committee is exploratory. It is fact-finding.
It is endeavouring to find out what is in everybody's
mind. It was decided at the Consultative Council—'

that was the Foreign Ministers—

'that the committee's report should come before
them at the next meeting. It is at this stage that the
governments will have to make their decisions as to what
is the best form in which to develop this organization.'

Our purpose, therefore, is to prepare the way for that
consideration by the governments.

.   .   .   .   .

We are in the midst of taking evidence and having
discussions among ourselves.

I now propose to say a few words about the declarations
of the Leader of the Opposition on this matter; this will
conveniently lead on to the quotations I intend to make
from what I myself have said. I do not disagree at all
with what I am now going to quote. It is reported in

The Times of November 18th that the right hon. Gentleman opened a United Europe Exhibition. The report said:

> 'Mr. Churchill said that to imagine that Europe to-day was ripe for either a political federation or a customs union would be wholly unrealistic.'

He rules out a federation and he rules out a customs union. At any rate, a customs union is now being studied by a body working under the Brussels Treaty. The difficulties of such a union for us without Commonwealth relationships are very great. That indeed is obvious. But the right hon. Gentleman goes further and he says that it would be wholly unrealistic. He says the same for a political federation. The report continues:

> 'But who could say what might not be possible in the future?'

The right hon. Gentleman will notice a curious similarity between those and some remarks of my own which I will quote in a moment.

Mr. CHURCHILL: Oh!

Mr. DALTON: I am very sorry for the right hon. Gentleman, but he will notice that in a moment. The right hon. Gentleman then went on to say:

> 'They should not underrate the progress already made in the field of inter-governmental co-operation during the last twelve months.'

I do not want to quote at undue length, but the right hon. Gentleman went on further to say:

> 'It might, of course, be argued that a purely deliberative Assembly without executive powers would develop into an irresponsible talking-shop, and that it would be better to leave the work of European unification to be achieved through inter-governmental negotiations.'

He said that was not true and dissented from that idea. It shows once again that he rejects federation and a customs union.

I have taken the precaution of bringing the official report

of what I said at the last Annual Conference of the Labour
Party. When accusations are made in vague terms and
without much detail as to my being an enemy of Western
Union and so forth, I always wait to hear exactly what
speech it is that is cited. I have a note of what was said by
the right hon. Gentleman the Member for Warwick and
Leamington yesterday. He cited a speech which I made in
May at Scarborough. Some of my hon. Friends heard that
speech, but naturally the Press were only able to report part
of it. It was a lengthy speech and I am going to quote
only a few bits of it. It was a winding-up speech at the end
of a fairly lively debate on a wide range of subjects including
federal union, common provisions for defence, and a project
for a Socialist United Europe. At the end, on behalf of
the National Executive of the Labour Party, I wound up.
I touched upon a number of these matters in what I have
to say. It has been stated in the *Continental Daily Mail*
that I am a notorious arch-enemy of Western Union.
The right hon. Gentleman the Member for Woodford does
not read the Press which supports the Opposition. He
ought to read the *Continental Daily Mail*. It has been saying
the most scandalous things.

Mr. CHURCHILL: I always do when I am in Paris. I get
it every day.

Mr. DALTON: I get it too, as a precaution.

I want to quote in order to put this matter in proper
focus. I always like to be judged by the words I spoke at
the time. These are the words I spoke at the time. I was
not a member of the government. I was speaking respon-
sibly and I said then just the same as I do now. I was
speaking on behalf of the National Executive of the Labour
Party winding up this debate. I am quoting from the
official report of the Labour Conference at Scarborough.
I said:

> '. . . this conception of the United States of Europe,
> which has been in the minds of imaginative and noble
> thinkers throughout many generations, is a constructive
> idea which rallies almost universal support when put in
> general terms. It is right that we should lift up our eyes

towards the high mountains from which we draw our hope. It is also important that we should keep our feet upon the ground in our approach to them.'

The phrase 'Feet on the ground' has now gone into the title of a document which has been issued from Transport House. Then I referred to what had already been done in very similar terms to the speech made by the right hon. Gentleman which I have just quoted. I referred to what had been done in regard to O.E.E.C. and the building up of that organization. I said:

'That organization is in existence and has begun to work.'

I described its constitution. I said:

'It has set up a Supreme Council of sixteen members representing the sixteen European countries who are going to participate in the European Recovery Programme.'

I said that the Executive Council consisted of seven members. I continued:

'The Secretary General is a distinguished Frenchman and an important secretariat and group of technical committees have been appointed. Those are facts and not aspirations. Therefore already the first steps have been taken towards the end that is universally desired. We should be glad that this is so, and I pay my tribute to the man who more than any other in this country is responsible for it, namely, Ernest Bevin, the Foreign Secretary, who has been organizing those forward steps.

Then I spoke of the federal possibilities which the right hon. Gentleman and I both agree are not for to-day. *I spoke of the alternative possibility of advancing step by step along what is called 'the functional road'.* I said:

'. . . you should begin by dealing with those things that are ripe to be dealt with through the agencies that exist.'

In the next sentence I used a phrase which I hope will not cause dismay to people with thin skins. I said:

'You should begin, not with conclaves of chatterboxes,

I

but with functional advances by governments who have the power to make their decisions operative. . . . Let those governments appoint their representatives and get on with the detailed actual first stages for the closer economic integration of Western Europe.'

I went on to say:

'I am wholly for the practical British functional approach rather than for any theoretical federalism. Let us keep our feet upon the ground. I certainly do not wish'

—and this is getting very close to what the right hon. Gentleman said—

'to rule out the possibility of federal developments later, when we see how we get on with the existing arrangements and what sort of people we might have to bring into a federal scheme.'

Mr. BOOTHBY (Aberdeen and Kincardine, East): May I ask the right hon. Gentleman whether he now thinks, looking back, if he had been successful in his attempt to sabotage what he called 'the conclave of chatterboxes at The Hague', it would have been a good thing?

Mr. DALTON: I think that has very little relevance to The Hague Conference. I think we attach very much more importance to what the governments have achieved, and I do not regard that as central to this controversy. After referring briefly to the question of joint defence, speaking at the end of a long debate, I said that no speaker had uttered a word of criticism against the Five-Power Treaty signed between the French, the three Benelux countries, and ourselves based upon the Pact of Brussels, in which we are all now in fact committed to join military arrangements with one another. I welcomed that and also its acceptance in the conference.

I now go on to cite what I said about the British Commonwealth, because this evidently has some connection with what I have said about Western Union. I said:

'We are very much closer, in all respects except distance, to Australia and New Zealand than we are to

Western Europe. Australia and New Zealand are populated by our kinsmen. They live under Labour Governments, they are democracies, they speak our language, they have high standards of life, and have the same political ideals as we have. If you go to those countries you find yourself at once completely at home in a way that you do not if you go to a foreign country as distinct from a British community overseas.'

I then spoke of Canada and South Africa, and then I said:

'I am quite sure if the choice were put to us: "Will you move closer to Western Europe at the cost of moving further away from the countries of the Commonwealth?" for my part I would answer: "No". If that were the choice, I would say: "If moving closer to Europe means moving further away from Australia and New Zealand and the rest, I do not move." However, I do not think that that is the dilemma. I think that we can move closer to Western Europe and at the same time maintain in all its fullness, and I hope perhaps extend and expand, our relationship with the countries of the Commonwealth.'

I continued by saying:

'The family is a closer unit'

—that is, the British family—

'but having said that, and on condition that we fully consult our comrades in the Commonwealth and carry them with us in our plans for closer connection with Western Europe, and making sure that these are not inimical to their interests, whether political or economic, by all means let us go forward.'

I do not find much evidence of sabotage in what I said then, and I went on to speak of what a federal system would mean, and the right hon. Gentleman agrees with me that this is wholly unrealistic, so that this could be called a hypothetical exercise. I thought it necessary to point out to the conference what it would mean, and I dwelt upon what we had achieved in the last three years in this country

—full employment, social security, and other things, and I said:

> 'We are not going to throw away the solid gains brought to us by a whole generation of political agitation and by the votes of our people and by three years of solid work in power in Parliament, in the trade unions, and in the government, upon any doctrinal altar of a federal Western Europe.'

It is perfectly clear that this passage of my speech is against precipitate federalism. There follows then the quotation which the right hon. Gentleman accurately gave yesterday in the context of a federal union.

Finally, I said, and I was referring to the extension of Socialist measures for planning and control:

> 'Without that we shall be doomed to go back again to the uncontrolled and unplanned capitalism and the uncontrolled and unplanned anti-social operations of financiers and vested interests; to go back to all those miseries we knew in the years between the wars.'

I apologize for quoting so much, but I have done so to put in its proper context what I then said, and from which, to-day, I withdraw not one word or sentence. We have a long way to go yet before we come up against this issue of federal union, which may endanger the livelihood of our people by leading to the handing over of the controls which we think are essential to us over a wide variety of things. We are a long way from that, and there is a great distance to be covered on that road.

I have made these remarks at length because I have been constantly attacked and have shown remarkable patience and reticence, but I think the time has come to get these matters put right. I hope to return to Paris in the course of next week, and we shall continue our work in a very friendly atmosphere with the French and Benelux representatives. We shall continue our efforts to make quite clear exactly what is implied in each of these schemes, so that we can put up to the government, not a lot of vague generalities, but some perfectly clear and detailed propositions, showing how this scheme or that scheme would work in practice. I believe that that will be found to be a very valuable and useful piece of work. I am quite satisfied that those associated with me could not have been better chosen for the work in hand.

That Mr. Dalton's views were not shared by all the rank and file of the Labour Party may be gathered from a broadcast by Mr. R. H. S. Crossman, M.P., printed in the *Listener* on January 13, 1949:

> . . . the solution of the German problem is to be found not in Germany but in Paris and Brussels and London. Belgian and French statesmen are pressing for a European Assembly as a first stage in the advance to a federal union. British statesmen are arguing for a functional approach which avoids directly tackling the fundamental political problem. But when we consider Germany we realize that political union is the only functional way of dealing with the German menace.
>
> The choice is clear. If we are determined each to retain our national sovereignty and make Western Union a union of sovereign States then within ten years the western German State will be strong enough to wield the balance of power in Europe and to begin the process of recreating the Reich. In that case the third world war is inevitable.

The issue between the federal and the functional approach was lucidly stated in a broadcast by Mr. W. N. Ewer, whose permission I have to reprint what he said.

Both Mr. Bevin's speech and the debate which followed ranged over a wide field, yet it was quite clear that there was one subject right in the front of everybody's mind— the problem of what the Foreign Secretary called building 'a solid structure' of co-operation between the democratic countries of Europe; of creating a new unity between nations that have so often, and so recently, engaged in devastating wars with each other.

Everybody agrees that there must be some such solid structure. But the trouble is that there's wide disagreement about how that solid structure can be built. We want a structure not just blueprints. Blueprints for some kind of European union aren't in the least new, they're anyway as old as the 'grand design' of Henry IV of France over three hundred years ago. The first really serious attempt at the creation of anything we should now regard as an international organization, was, of course, the foundation of the League of Nations after the 1914–18 war. But there's a big difference; the character of the problem had in one way completely changed. Previously men had thought in terms of a purely European organization, some kind of alliance, even federation, between the States of Europe. But by 1918 it had become obvious that this, in itself, would be completely inadequate either as a guarantee of peace or as an instrument of economic and other co-operation; a European organization wouldn't be enough— nothing short of a world organization could deal with the problems created by a world war. It wasn't just that questions of power and security and balance of power, and the like, were now world-wide, but the economy of all the European countries had become an integral part of world economy. Their industries were dependent on supplies of food and raw materials from the other continents, and on the marketing of their products in those continents.

Europe, by reason of its own expansion, was no longer in any way self-contained. And yet—and yet the feeling that somehow or other in spite of all this there was still some sort of unity, some sort of homogeneity between the European countries, or at any rate the West-European countries, which differentiated them from the rest of the world, that feeling did still persist and, of course, it expressed itself in Briand's abortive plan twenty-five years ago now for a United States of Europe. It's far stronger to-day, and that's a good reason. For one reason the economy of the countries of Western Europe has been more disrupted and dislocated than ever before, they've become economically more dis-united than they ever were. And even to get back to the—something like the old kind of economic relations which existed between them before the war, would require joint effort and joint reorganization. And—and we passed at the same time, under the same pressure of hard economic facts into a period in which the economies of all these countries are, to a greater or less degree, planned economies. Restoring their economic relations isn't any longer just a question of removing trade barriers, it's a question of fitting together planned economies; and for that some kind of organization is quite clearly essential. Now the second stimulus to unity is paradoxically—regrettably—the existence of a deep dis-unity. Europe to-day is completely and sharply divided into east and west. It's an inescapable though an unpleasant fact—the 'two camps' of Communist theory do to-day exist in fact. The nations of Western Europe are confronted by the existence of a solid disciplined *bloc* of East-European States under Soviet leadership. And the Western nations feel themselves and their institutions to be menaced. They feel that their security is, at any rate, potentially in danger and they feel that security can only be achieved by unity in the face of a common peril.

So the urge to closer unity between the Western democratic nations is stronger than it's ever been before, the need for it is almost universally admitted; the issue is decided in principle. The problem is how to achieve it in practice and it is an intensely difficult one.

Now there are roughly two schools of thought which one may label for convenience, federalist and functionalist. The federalists hold that nothing will be any use short of the creation of a federal State or federal united States, in which the different countries would cease to be sovereign independent States and would become component parts of a single whole, though with a large measure of self-government for each of them. They argue that all efforts to achieve really close co-operation between completely independent governments are just doomed to failure, that national interests and nationalist feelings will always wreck them; that the need for securing unanimity will always prevent the working out of any really effective schemes, or effective plans. Either there will be disagreement, which will prevent anything from being done at all, or there will be half-hearted compromises which will be totally ineffective, which won't work and will simply create new confusions and new quarrels. Nothing, then, the federalists say, but the existence of a federal government and a federal parliament with full powers to take and to enforce binding decisions over the whole area of the federation; nothing but that will be able to achieve the desired results—nothing short of it will be a solid structure, nothing else will provide either security or the possibility of economic recovery. And therefore we ought to direct our efforts, not to the creation of what they regard as a complicated unworkable machinery of co-operation between governments; but to the creation, as rapidly as possible, of a single government with full sovereign powers responsible through a single parliament to a single European electorate. Of course, its powers would be defined, and in many matters the component States would still be fully self-governing.

But in all that there's a common concern, especially in such all important matters as defence, finance, economic planning—the federal authority would be supreme.

Now that's the federalist view. The functionalist reply is, in effect, that this is magnificent but that it's not practical. They don't believe that at the moment there's the remotest chance of the peoples of the different countries agreeing to accept so vast a change. They don't believe that the people of this country, for example, would agree to have the planning of their economic life carried out by a government which would be preponderantly foreign. They don't believe that the people of this country, or any other, would agree to have all the vital issues over which we quarrel between ourselves decided, as it were, over our heads by foreign votes in a European parliament. And they fear that any attempt to enforce the decrees of a federal authority on a reluctant nation, would lead to resistance, to a passionate demand for repeal, for the restoration of national independence.

This—this sudden and almost artificial creation of a new super-State would bring about not any real unity but would even intensify antagonisms and quarrels; and perhaps—perhaps even bring about civil wars.

They fear that a federal parliament would simply be a complex jigsaw puzzle of nationalities and parties, that it would inevitably break up into small and quarrelling groups, and, in fact, there wouldn't be a hope of its producing a firm and stable majority which could carry through big projects or make consistent plans. And they suspect that a federal government, similarly divided, would in practice turn out to be feeble, and incompetent. In a word, they fear the federation would produce, not unity but disunity; not strength but weakness. That we shall have destroyed the strength and efficiency of the national governments and should have put in their place, not something stronger and more efficient, but something which would, of its very nature, be feeble and inefficient, and quite possibly doomed to a speedy collapse. In which case our last state would be very much worse than our first. Therefore they suggest that the right line of approach isn't to attempt now to set up any kind of federal machinery or federal authority, but to devote ourselves to the less spectacular but more practical, and as they see it more profitable, job of creating and developing the machinery of closer co-operation between the existing governments and the existing authorities.

They want to continue a process which has already been started by the creation of the Organization for European Economic Co-operation and by the creation of the Western Union by the five Brussels Treaty Powers. By the same process developing more and more, they see—they see various peoples, the various political leaders, becoming more and more used to the idea, and more and more accustomed to the practice of working together, and of using voluntarily majority decisions until, by a sort of organic growth, the stage would be reached at which, in Mr. Bevin's words, 'The defence ministers and finance ministers of the Western world would be discussing a common budget with a common method of defence.' And from that, perhaps in due course, there would evolve a real federal structure, far more real and far stronger than anything created suddenly, overnight, from blueprints. Well, that's the functionalists' case.

Now at the moment the division between federalists and functionalists is showing itself in their attitude towards the first tentative steps which are being suggested for the establishment of some kind of organization which would, at any rate, symbolize the desired European unity. The federalists, and those who partially share their ideas, want now to set up a European Assembly chosen, not by the governments but by the parliaments of various countries. Most of them agree that for the moment such an assembly shouldn't have any actual power, it should only be able to discuss and to make recommendations. But it would be representative, not of the governments but of the peoples; and they look to its developing into a real European parliament. They hope, indeed, that such an assembly would, itself, take the lead in pushing forward the whole idea of federation, and would assert its own influence against those of the national governments and parliaments.

Now Mr. Bevin, speaking on December 9th, was quite frank in opposing this idea. Such a body, with neither power nor responsibility, would, he suggested, be a mere façade, a thing that could do nothing and stop at that. It would merely lead to another disappointment. Now that does not mean that he's unwilling to do anything more at present, but his idea is rather that there should be, not an assembly without either power or responsibility, but a Council of Europe which, though it might not at present have any power, would, at any rate, have responsibility, because it would be composed of ministers and delegates chosen by an able speaker on behalf of their governments. He sees it, I think, as something between a sort of miniature United Nations Organization dealing with specifically European problems and a council of the type which was set up by the five States of the Brussels Treaty. I think he envisages committees of defence ministers and their advisers to deal with defence, finance ministers and their advisers to deal with financial matters, and so on. Not a debating body but a body, or perhaps a network of bodies, concentrating on the working out of practical problems. This choice between a parliamentary assembly and a sort of governmental council is now being discussed and considered in the Five-Power Committee in Paris. It may be, of course we can't tell yet, that the committee may recommend setting up both. But behind that immediate question there lies all the time a deeper and more difficult question—'Are we going to move to the goal of union by the federal or by the functional approach?'

Well, I've tried to set up a case for those, but the choice has got to be made, and it's one on which we will all very soon have to make up our own minds.

PART III

WORLD REVOLUTION

ESSENTIALS OF THE SCHEME

XVI

THE KEY TO THE PROBLEM

MR. DALTON'S speeches had left the impression that Western Union was of interest to him as a means whereby Europe could be brought to accept a Socialist policy. Public opinion, divided on the question of socialism, agreed that the 'one thing which mattered to-day was the prevention of war', and was not reassured to find that His Majesty's Government had entrusted the policy directed to that end to one who seemed to think that socialism was of greater importance than peace. At the turn of the year it looked as though the arguments of M. Ramadier and M. Spaak had made some impression on Mr. Dalton, for the Press stated that the Conference would submit to their governments a combination of the British with the French and Belgian proposals. This was quickly followed by a further announcement that Mr. Bevin had postponed the consideration of the compromise until he had discussed it with the French Prime Minister, who was coming to visit him in London on January 12th. On January 4th the Paris Correspondent of *The Times* reported that the British note to M. Schuman asked for 'a postponement of several weeks of the meeting which was to have taken place on Thursday' (January 6th). It would thus seem impossible to have anything ready for the meeting of the Foreign Ministers of the Brussels Treaty Powers on January 26th, and another three months would go by before the ministers could meet again to come to any decision about a European Assembly and Council.

There is no doubt that the British suggestion, however good the reasons for making it, must rekindle in French minds the earlier misgivings about the sincerity of the present British approach to European unity.

The wish to see the early establishment of joint European bodies, particularly an assembly, has become more and more manifest in France in the last few months, and the reaction to this latest development cannot be other than one of disappointment and anxiety.

The following statement was issued by the secretary-general of the Brussels Treaty permanent commission at the end of the ministers' discussions.

The fourth meeting of the Consultative Council took place in London on January 27th and 28th.

The Council took note with satisfaction of the work accomplished under the Brussels Treaty in the social and cultural spheres. A detailed statement on social and cultural matters is attached.

After considering the most valuable preparatory work accomplished in Paris by the Committee for the Study of European Unity, the Council agreed that there should be established a Council of Europe, consisting of a ministerial committee, meeting in private, and a consultative body, meeting in public.

The permanent commission was instructed to study the detailed application of the decisions of principle taken by the Council.

The Council decided to invite other European countries to take part in negotiations for the establishment of the Council of Europe.

The Council also considered a report on matters relating to defence, and there was a useful interchange of views on certain outstanding political matters.

As regards Palestine, there was general agreement that the stage had now been reached at which *de facto* recognition could be given to the Government of Israel.

So much for the present; and now for the future. Let us waste no time on picturing difficulties to be met, but try to see how past experience can be used to bring this World Revolution to its end. If we hold in mind that to prevent war is the one thing which matters, we shall not be drawn into those bypaths where governments have wandered since hostilities ceased.

We are now standing at the very point where those who were trying to end the American Revolution stood in 1787. They had realized that the functional approach, the attempt to end the revolution by gradual and imperceptible steps, by 'a creeping and incipient union', had merely raised 'an insuperable jealousy' in the sovereign governments. They faced the fact that these sovereign governments had proved themselves unable to relieve the American people from the fear of impending war. They saw that this could only be done by putting the task of preserving peace on the shoulders of the whole American people. They drafted a document showing how this could be done, and placed it before the American people to accept or reject. They were then surprised by its prompt and enthusiastic acceptance. Perhaps they were even more surprised to see how the fear of war began to subside as soon as the people of the United States had once for all taken on themselves the task of preventing war by electing a government charged with the duty of taking the necessary measures on their behalf, and also equipped with the powers necessary for that task.

K

We can now see that nothing short of the adoption by the electorates of a written constitution could have banished the fear of war which the functional approach had only deepened.

Had we time to review the measures taken under Washington's presidency we should also see how the economic, social, and legal problems, which had proved intractable so long as the fear of war prevailed, began to find their solutions. In politics there are no panaceas. It is none the less true that at times one outstanding question forbids an answer to all others until it is solved. Such a question is now the prevention of war. Attempts to repair the ravages of two catastrophic wars, to restore industry and trade, or effect social reform, will lead only to greater confusion in the world so long as it feels that an even yet more terrible war awaits it in the future. When once this fear is removed effective solutions of secondary problems will then be possible.

These fruits of experience are not confined to a century and half of American history. Their seed has since been replanted in Switzerland, Canada, Australia, and South Africa, and have there yielded a similar harvest. The founders of the U.S.A. were in the fullest sense pioneers, who found their way through an unknown country. Though our task is as much greater than theirs as the world is greater than America, these pioneers have left their footprints for us to follow. We shall end the World Revolution, as they ended the American Revolution, only when our leaders have prepared an international constitution and have laid it before us ordinary people to accept or to reject. The problems of reconstruction, of economic and social reform, will then begin to find effective and lasting solutions, and not till then.

This truth was stated by Churchill when, in eloquent words, he described the conditions which prevail to-day over the greater part of Europe as:

A horrible retrogression back to the Middle Ages, without their chivalry, without their faith. *Yet all this could be ended in a single stroke.* Two or three hundred millions of people in Europe have only got to wake up one morning and resolve to be happy and free by becoming one family of nations, banded together from the Atlantic to the Black Sea for mutual aid and protection. *One spasm of resolve!* One single gesture! The prison doors clang open. Out walk, or totter, the captives into the sunshine of a joyous world.

Has a greater promise ever been offered by a practical statesman to a suffering world? How long must it wait for overworked statesmen to nerve themselves to 'one spasm of resolve' and take that 'single stroke'? But whenever the statesmen of two or more nations sit down to draft a constitution for an international democracy, it is vital to the interests of mankind that the instrument should be so framed that more backward nations, as they advance and learn how to govern themselves, will find it easy for them to join the international State. For this and other reasons it is all important that British statesmen should take their part in drafting the first constitution for an international democracy; for they, more than others, have known what it is to deal with a quarter of the human race, in every continent, of every race, and of every level of civilization. And the International Convention will find how important it is to have an agenda in which the questions to be answered are arranged in the right order.

XVII

THE INTERNATIONAL CONVENTION: IMPORTANCE OF ITS AGENDA

THE task of drafting the first constitution of an international democracy will not prove so difficult as it now seems, if at every turn the draftsmen remember that the paramount object to be kept in view is to remove the fear of another war. By holding in mind this aim they will find the key to every problem. They will also find themselves producing a short and conservative instrument, but one capable of expansion, as experience may suggest when it has come into effect.

The first problems to be faced will be how to distribute (1) the burden of the common defence, and (2) representation on the federal legislature between the nations which join the union. If the two questions are dealt with in that order, a wise answer to the first will provide an answer to the second.

As to the first, the draftsmen should recall the principle upon which the cost of defence is distributed between taxpayers in their own country. To distribute the cost of defence in proportion to the benefit received by each taxpayer is impossible. It must, therefore, be distributed in proportion to the ability of each taxpayer to bear the burden, on what Adam Smith called the basis of taxable capacity. For a national treasurer to assess the taxable capacity of millions of taxpayers is no easy task. He does his best and replies to critics that 'government is a rough business'.

In the light of modern statistics, the taxable capacity of a whole nation can be measured with greater accuracy than the taxable capacity of its numerous taxpayers. An international commission of financial experts would have no difficulty in assessing the relative taxable capacities of two or more nations, and could also revise their assessment, say every five years, with increasing accuracy. The total cost of defence could then be distributed between the national treasuries on this scientific basis. Under the constitution the quota due from each nation should be made payable by the national bank holding the consolidated fund of each constituent State, on requisition by the federal bank, without further authority from the national legislatures. It would be the constitutional duty of the national legislatures to see that their consolidated fund was sufficient to meet the federal requisition as well as the cost of their own national services. If the requisition was refused, or the consolidated fund was inadequate to meet it, the federal government should then be authorized to apply to the Supreme Court of the Union for an order giving the federal officers power to collect from the national customs and excise of the defaulting State enough money to meet the requisition. If these sources should prove inadequate, the federal government should then be empowered by the court to impose and collect direct taxation on the taxpayers of the defaulting State. To resist the collection of such taxes would then be an act of secession for which no constitution can provide. The issue would have to be met, as Lincoln met the secession of the southern States, by calling the federal army into action to enforce the constitution as interpreted by the court.

Under this arrangement the distribution of all public burdens between one taxpayer and another would rest where it now rests, with each national government. The draftsmen would realize the advantage of this when they came to decide the line of division between the federal and State functions. Here especially they will do well to hold in mind that the paramount reason for the federal union is to establish forces by land, sea, and air too strong for any aggressor to attack. They must give the federal government all the powers required for that purpose. All other powers should be reserved to States; that is, to existing national governments. Their fields should cover domestic affairs. We return to this all important subject later.

If the burden of defence is distributed in accordance with the taxable capacity of each State in the Union to be defended, it is reasonable that control of expenditure should be distributed amongst those States on the same principle. The capacity of the first international constitution, which must be framed by the experienced democracies, to include backward peoples as they learn to govern themselves, will depend on whether representation in the federal legislature is based on population or on taxable capacity. At The Hague Conference —which only sat for four days—there was no time to discuss this question and the basis of population was assumed. If that basis is accepted in the constitution a dangerous crisis will arise whenever more backward nations like China, Japan, or those of Africa have acquired a sufficient capacity to govern themselves and apply for admission to the Union. The experienced democracies who have founded the Union will find that to admit a people so numerous as the Chinese will at

once place Chinese in control of the federal government. The danger would be increased by the fact that
the founder States with their higher taxable capacity
would still be bearing the major cost of defence. They
would certainly refuse to take the risk. They would,
indeed, be mad to do so. The result will be insuperable
division between the advanced and backward races.
The colour bar would be raised as a wall of partition
across the world.

While we may hope and expect that in course of time
politicially backward peoples like the Chinese will
learn to keep order amongst themselves, it is most
unlikely that they will ever achieve the same taxable
capacity per head as the nations of Western Europe,
the United States, or the British Dominions. If in the
first constitution the representation of States is based
on taxable capacity, the problem in generations to
come of admitting the numerous peoples of Asia and
Africa will be reduced to manageable shape. The
experienced democracies who have formed the Union
will not be faced by the danger of suddenly handing
over control of the federal government and of its
treasury to less experienced and far more numerous
peoples. Indeed, in the case of China or Africa, their
representation based on taxable capacity might be so
low as to demand that some weight should be given to
the factor of population. The constitution should be
so framed as to admit of some reasonable compromise
whenever the occasion arises. But suddenly to swamp
the experienced democracies by admitting the Chinese
on the basis of population would be midsummer
madness.

XVIII

DISTRIBUTION OF FUNCTIONS

THE third problem to be solved is what powers to vest in the federal authority and what others to reserve to the national governments of the States. Here again the question can be answered if the draftsmen keep in mind defence as the primary object of the Union. The federal government must have power to create and maintain forces by land, sea, and air too strong for any aggressor to challenge. The field left to the national governments of the States will then be so wide as to include the control of all their national and domestic affairs. In drawing the line between federal and State powers the experience of British statesmen, and still more those of the Dominions, will be found of capital importance. In the British Commonwealth the Dominions have, in fact, complete and final control of national and domestic affairs. They have, on paper, control of the issues of peace and war, but on paper only.

Their control of their own domestic affairs is real and effective, because Dominion governments are handling what they understand and can manage much better than any authority in Downing Street or Westminster, even if that authority were based on the representation of all the countries concerned. They exercise final control not only of their own social structure, but also (and this is of even greater importance) of its composition. They have, and they exercise, the right to exclude immigrants. If they had not had this right Canada, Australia, New Zealand, and South Africa would each have become colonies of Asia or Africa, or of both. These democracies would never consent to hand over the power to control migration to an international government and would be mad to do so. The American States, of course, assigned this power to the Federal Government, and Americans who have not studied Dominion experience are apt to assume that in any international union the power to control migration must belong to the federal government. But when confronted with the question whether to accept a constitution under which the international government would have the power to open North America to immigration from Asia, they would instantly, and rightly, refuse to accept a change which would add to their colour problem the racial complications which distract the South African Union.

If national governments are to retain effective control of domestic affairs, they must retain their present control of taxation in all its forms. The paramount duty of a government which controls domestic affairs is to adjust the relations of rich and poor. Taxation is the instrument by which this is done. No government can adjust the relations of rich and poor unless it controls indirect as well as direct taxation. Here again the experience of the British Commonwealth cannot be ignored. The Dominions have long acquired absolute control of their own customs.

On the eve of the national conference which drafted the constitution of the South African Union, H. A. L. Fisher remarked in a lecture that 'such projects had succeeded where draftsmen had been careful to avoid embarrassing and inflammatory matter'. On December 29, 1948, at a conference of the Council for Education in World-Citizenship Sir David Wailey, speaking on Economic European Co-operation, said that the detrimental effect of trade barriers had been unduly exaggerated. They had not been created merely out of perversity, and although the beggar-my-neighbour attitude of international trade was to be deplored, the history of a thousand years could not be reversed in a few months. The anxiety to vest the control of customs in a federal government of Western Union is a typical example of 'embarrassing and inflammatory matter'.

I cannot conceive that either the Dominions or the U.S.A. will enter a union under a constitution which deprives them of power to control their own tariff or migration laws. On the other hand, I think they would join a union if its first constitution provides only for the defence, and functions inseparable therefrom, the control of foreign affairs, of dependencies, and of air routes between the countries which belong to the Union. I think that the U.S.A. will join when they see that the Union for common defence is removing the risk and the fear of war.

In the British Commonwealth as now constituted the power of Dominion governments to control migration and tariffs has complicated the task of the British Government in seeking to avert war. Let us face the fact that the tariff and migration laws of the Dominions were the main factors in bringing Japan, our ally in War I, to join our enemies in War II. The efforts of the so-called Imperial Government to persuade Dominion governments to modify features of their laws objectionable to Asiatics had little effect. The reasons for this are not far to seek. The Imperial Government was imperial only in respect of its responsibility for the issues of peace and war, but not in its powers to remove the causes of war. It represents only the people of the British Isles, and not those of the Dominions. Dominion governments had all the powers but, except on paper, no real responsibility for maintaining the peace, and were slow to realize that if war broke out they, no less than Britain, would be drawn into it. Incredible as it now seems in the light of the last war, Australia did not contribute one penny to the fortification of Singapore. All but a fraction of the cost was met by British taxpayers on the other side of the world. It must, however, be added that Australia has since made gifts to Britain which exceed the amount that British taxpayers spent on Singapore before the war. These sums do not include gifts of food to the British people which Australians have made and are still making with unparalleled generosity.

The position of an international government would be immeasurably stronger in this respect than that of the Imperial Government as it now is. It would represent the Dominion peoples no less than the British people. Its executive as well as its legislature would include representatives from the Dominions, who would help the federal government to convince their own people if the peace of the Union was imperilled by unreasonable tariffs and migration laws. The Union Government would be in a position to offer Dominion governments inducements to modify laws offensive to other powers. The Union Government will have to establish dockyards and arsenals to produce munitions, especially in its more distant States. Countries like South Africa and Australia will greatly desire to secure the location of such arsenals and dockyards in their own territories, and will, therefore, be more willing to meet reasonable requests of the federal government to keep their tariff and migration laws within moderate bounds.

There are thus strong reasons why the constitution should leave the control of tariffs and migration with the national governments where they now rest. If in course of time experience should prove that the final control of such matters should be vested in the federal government it can then be done by amending the constitution. For that reason amendment should be made easier than it is under the American Constitution. I believe, however, that experience of the working of an international commonwealth would convince everyone that the States must retain their control of tariffs and migration.

The proposal to start with a customs union is due to more than one cause. It shows that its authors have forgotten that the primary object of union is to prevent war. It also shows that they have forgotten that the States which Americans had to unite were, in fact, adjacent provinces, and not nations some of which are divided by oceans. It is prompted by the predisposition of its authors for the functional approach, for putting the cart before the horse. The movement for Western Union will never succeed until it is realized that economic problems are not the key to political problems, and that political problems with all their thorns must be firmly grasped and settled before we can hope to deal with economic and social problems. The functional approach, like the policy of appeasement, is the course of the least resistance, the broad and downward road which leads to destruction. We shall follow that fatal path until some minister in office can nerve himself to lead us up the straight and narrow way, to peace and safety.

We have still to deal with the question whether the federal government or the State governments should control merchant shipping, passports, and the coining of money.

As to merchant shipping we have to consider its strategic as well as its economic aspect. In time of peace merchant ships are for the most part built, owned, and operated by private owners. In time of war merchant ships are as essential to victory as warships. Japan had foreseen this after the first war. By playing off against each other the conflicting interests of Great Britain, India, Australia, and New Zealand, Japan succeeded in reducing British tonnage in the East by over 1,500,000 tons. In War II we had 2,000 fewer vessels than in War I. Japanese tonnage had grown from 1,500,000 tons to over 5,000,000. Japanese ships were carrying 73 per cent of British trade in the Far East. The ships which enabled Japan to conquer our Eastern Empire and to threaten Australia, New Zealand, and India, and even South Africa, were largely paid for by producers and merchants under the British flag.

In Chapter XVII we have said that the federal government must have all the powers necessary to provide for the defence of the Union on a scale that no aggressor will dare to challenge. Power to secure that the Union has all the merchant ships it would need if war were to break out is clearly implicit in the grant of such powers. If the cost of federal defence is a first charge on the revenues of the Union the federal government will be able to give effect to such powers.

We may now turn to the economic aspect of merchant shipping in time of peace. In the British Commonwealth the Dominions exercise exactly the same control as the United Kingdom so far as the law governing shipping is concerned. There is now no law which governs the shipping of the Commonwealth as a whole. The Dominions are free to regulate their shipping as best suits their different national conditions, and this could continue in an international union. The federal government must always be on the watch to see whether in the event of a sudden attack by some irresponsible dictator the States of the Union have merchant shipping enough for all the purposes of war. If at any time the federal government considers that more shipping would be needed to meet these purposes, then under its comprehensive power to do everything necessary for defence it can arrange and pay for the construction of additional ships needed to render the Union immune from risk of attack.

Federalist writers, who are given to travel, commonly assume that passports between States members of the Union will disappear. If the reasons urged in Chapter XVIII against depriving States of their power to control migration are valid, they must also retain power to grant or refuse passports and visas. This dream of abolishing passports is another example of the tendency to forget that the object of the Union is to create a system of international defence which will end the fear of war. Nations will not consent to merge their national sovereignties merely to serve the convenience of travellers.

People who have to travel know that the major inconvenience is caused not by passports, but by currency restrictions. If, as in Chapter XVII, all powers necessary for defence are assigned to the federal government it will not be necessary to assign power to coin money. The federal government will have to pay millions to soldiers, sailors, and airmen all over the world. In order to do this it would have to create a federal currency. There is no need to deprive the State governments of power to continue their own national currencies if they like to do so. But in all likelihood these national currencies would fade out of existence when the federal currency had become available to industry and commerce. The convenience of travellers would also be met.

XIX

WHY NATIONAL GOVERNMENTS ARE NOW THREATENED WITH BREAKDOWN

TILL the close of 1947 this country was following the easy and downward road which was fast leading to national bankruptcy. Our credit abroad had sunk to its lowest level. Addressing a gathering of physicists Sir Stafford Cripps uttered a warning which does not seem to have reached the ears of those who forget that unless peace is established in time it may not be established at all.

> World federation has hitherto been looked upon as a very long term objective, but the atomic bomb has telescoped history and made it impossible for us to wait long years of acute danger of war, because from the war civilization and mankind cannot survive. We may have a few years yet in which the atomic bomb is not a common weapon in the hands of all major powers, but they will be pitifully few compared to the immense task that confronts us.

In the closing days of 1947 the decline of our national credit was arrested by the appointment of Sir Stafford Cripps as Chancellor of the Exchequer. His achievement in twelve months was recorded by the *Economist* on Christmas Day, 1948, in the following words:

> There can be no doubt that, on the major issues of economic policy, the nation has been travelling during 1948 on the right road. Indeed, the best way of realizing what a distance has been travelled is to look back to Christmas,

1947, and to observe the almost magical change that has occurred in that sensitive barometer of national standing, the prestige and position of the pound sterling. A year ago the pound was shunned and suspect; now it is among the world's hard currencies. Then the world's criticism was that the British economy was incapable of paying its way; now it is that British policy is aiming at making the pound too scarce. This change is not entirely one of psychology and atmosphere; it has been produced by the restraint that has been shown in British spending abroad and the energy that has been shown in the export drive. When the figures of the current balance of payments come to be published, it is expected that they will show an overall balancing of payment and receipts, without the aid of Marshall dollars— that is to say, they will show a surplus in all other currencies approximately equal to the continuing deficit in dollars. This is a great achievement by any test, and though the ultimate credit belongs to the British people's capacity for self-control, by far the greatest individual share of praise attaches to Sir Stafford Cripps and the small circle of his intimate advisers. Not only has he shaped the policies and tenaciously defended them, he has also provided the essential moral foundation. A people that is being asked to exercise such severe self-discipline must be convinced that what is asked of it is asked for the good of the community, not to flatter the vanity or foster the ambition of a politician. This confidence Sir Stafford has created in full measure.

We who have followed the labours of Sir Stafford during this year, and have read the speeches in which he moved the people to accept his austere policy, may wonder how a man not born with the strength of a Hercules could survive such an effort. The essential cause of the bankruptcy from which he has saved us is failure to arrest the ever increasing drift to a third war. In the coming year we may hope that this weary Titan may find the strength to remind us, and his

L

colleagues, that our credit can never be stabilized while peace is left to hang by a thread.

This constant tendency to overlook the condition which underlies all our difficulties is, I believe, mainly due to a system which imposes on ministers burdens greater than anyone can bear. This is specially true in our own case of the Prime Minister, the Foreign Secretary, and the Chancellor of the Exchequer. The three years I spent in Whitehall in government service were terrifying. It was often my duty to attend Cabinet meetings and to see decisions taken, on which the issues of peace or war might hang, by ministers who had no time to study the information on which such decisions should be based. A system which imposes on a few ministers more work than a human being, however gifted, can do is, I believe, the main factor which has brought the world to its present pass. In the last century mechanization has increased beyond all knowledge the number of questions which no one but ministers can decide. The only possible division is one which draws a line between the functions proper to a national government and those which an inter-national government alone can discharge.

It is just such a line which must be drawn when national States unite for their common defence. They must establish a government responsible to all their peoples, equipped with the powers necessary to organize and maintain a system of defence so strong that no other power will dream of attacking them.

The federal government must control external affairs as well as defence. All other functions can then be reserved to national governments, whose ministers will at last find they have time to handle them, relieved as they will be of all concern for defence and foreign affairs. It is this over-burdening of national governments in modern democracies which has made them powerless to keep pace with social reform. When once those governments have time to deal with what they know and understand they will overtake these dangerous arrears in social reform. They will find they have not lost, but gained control of their own affairs—of those that are really their own.

Enough has been said in the three last chapters to show how disastrous it will be for the future of the world if British and Dominion ministers stand aside from a convention to draft the constitution of the first international commonwealth. If the ministers of Western Europe meet without British and Dominion ministers their tendency will be to follow too closely the model of the American Constitution. Since 1787 the British Commonwealth has accumulated a wealth of experience of which full use should be made in drafting a constitution which should in course of time come to include nations in every part of the world until at last it attains the stature of a world government.

There is no reluctance on the part of the nations of Europe to discuss the project of Western Europe with the British. On the contrary, they are looking for a lead from us. At The Hague Conference there was nothing more evident than the disposition of the nations there represented to regard Churchill as their saviour and to treat him as the leader of Europe. Our position in this matter rests on the fact universally recognized that throughout nine centuries British statesmen have been the architects of that system of freedom which nations in all continents have twice in this twentieth century fought to preserve. A system under which human society is divided into more than sixty sovereign States has palpably broken down. To end this World Revolution we must, in the words of Canning, call in the new world to redress the balance of the old. *We only* can utter that call, and if we refuse to make it we shall then betray our nature and our name.

It is no less important to remember that the men who drafted the American Constitution, such as Washington, Hamilton, and Madison, were mainly responsible for carrying it into effect, and seeing that it worked. It is obvious that men who take a leading part in drafting the constitution of an international commonwealth will find themselves in its government when it comes into being. If British ministers hold aloof from the convention they will find no place in the first international government, and their absence will be disastrous.

XX

CONTROL OF DEPENDENCIES

FOR strategic reasons the control of defence cannot be separated from control of dependencies. Our experience in the last war of Palestine, of Dakar, the maintenance of air routes across Africa, and of Madagascar has proved this beyond dispute. In an international union the control of colonies must pass from the States that join it to the international government. This means that at last the Belgian Congo and the French and British colonies of tropical Africa would be brought under one authority. One government would control tropical Africa south of the Sudan to the Zambesi. The control of the Dutch East Indies would also pass to that government. The world would have reached a system under which the peoples who are trying to do their duty to the backward races could at last do it with the best intentions. They are each trying to solve the colour problem in their own way. When one authority is based on the creed that self-government cannot remain the monopoly of the white races the colour problem will begin to find its solution. One negro dominion can be built up from the Zambesi to the Sahara and its people trained in the task of governing themselves. Then at last will be realized the prophetic words in which Pitt supported the motion by Wilberforce to abolish the slave trade. The debate had lasted till seven o'clock in the morning and as Pitt was speaking rays of the rising sun broke through the windows of the House of Commons. His speech closed with these words:

> If we listen to the voice of reason and duty, and pursue this day the line of conduct which they prescribe, some of us may live to see the reverse of that picture from which we now turn our eyes with shame and regret. We may live to behold the natives of Africa engaged in the calm occupations of industry, in the pursuit of a just and legitimate commerce. We may behold the beams of science and philosophy breaking in upon their land, which, at some happy period, in still later times, may blaze with full lustre, and, joining their influence with that of pure religion, may illuminate and invigorate the most distant extremities of that immense continent. Then may we hope that even Africa, though last of all the quarters of the globe, shall enjoy in the evening of her days those blessings which have descended so plentifully upon us—
>
> > 'Nosque ubi primus equis Oriens adflavit anhelis
> > Illic sera rubens accendit lumina Vesper.'
>
> > 'And when upon us Dawn first breathed with panting steeds,
> > There, rosy evening kindled late her torches.'
>
> It is in this view, Sir; it is as an atonement for our long and cruel injustice towards Africa, that the measure proposed by my honourable friend most forcibly recommends itself to my mind.

XXI

THE SETTLEMENT OF GERMANY

THE creation of an international government will at once open doors to the solution of other and more immediate problems. Three years after hostilities ceased the victors have failed to ratify a single treaty of peace with the conquered nations. Since the last shot was fired in 1945 we are no nearer making peace with Germany, Austria, Italy, and Japan. Too many cooks have spoiled the broth of peace. Having pooled their forces under one command and won the war at immeasurable cost the victors are still unable to make peace with the nations they conquered. What further proof do we need that a league of sovereign States can combine to win a war, but cannot combine to prevent one happening? The sovereign democracies of the British Commonwealth have proved this twice in the present century.

It is tragic indeed that German goodwill, earned for the British and American peoples by their efforts to save Germany west of the Elbe from Russian oppression and to feed Berlin by air, is now being wiped out by the failure of the British, French, and American Governments to place Western Germany on a footing which would restore the self-respect of its people. Germany will always be a. menace to peace until its peoples have learned to govern themselves. The settlement of Germany would be simple, if it were placed in the hands of one real international government responsible to the peace-loving peoples of the West. Such a government would draw its authority from the British, French, Belgian, and Dutch electorates and, one hopes, from those of the Dominions, Scandinavia, and of Switzerland. These nations would have become States in one federation, but would also retain absolute control of their own domestic affairs. The German States, Hanover, Württemberg, Bavaria, and so on, are commensurate in size with countries like Belgium, Holland, and those of Scandinavia. If these German States were included as federal States on a footing of equality with experienced democracies, they would learn how to govern themselves as they never will by listening to lectures from us. Harnessed between experienced democracies in a federal government, they will learn how to apply self-government to their own domestic affairs.

The federal government would control all forces by land, sea, and air which could be used in another war. The States, as in America, would have their police and such forces of militia as are needed to maintain internal order; but those forces would not be equipped with artillery, tanks, or planes. The manufacture of all such weapons would be under the strict control of the federal authority. Such rearmament as took place in Germany under the Nazi régime would be impossible. The German States in control of domestic affairs would in time learn to value peace as other democracies have done, and would lose their present obsession for war. As things now are a great mass of the German people have so little belief in any solution not based on force that they think that their relations with Russia can only be settled by another war. As they learn how to govern themselves they will come to see that Bismarck was right in saying that one can do anything with bayonets but sit on them. With a federal government in absolute control of the issues of peace and war, and of all forces that can be used in war, the control of the Ruhr and its industries would become comparatively simple. Its production of coal and steel could be developed, without fear, for the benefit of all Europe. A task so great as the settlement of Germany can only be accomplished when those with whom it rests have created an instrument properly designed for the purpose.

That task, of course, cannot be complete so long as Russia controls millions of Germans east of the Elbe. As they see their compatriots west of that river controlling their own domestic affairs on a footing of equality with the Western democracies and recovering their self-respect, even Moscow will find that it cannot remain seated on bayonets. The iron curtain cannot conceal from their German helots the growing prosperity and happiness of their western compatriots, living side by side and on a footing of equality with the free and highly industrialized nations of the West, provided always that the Union in which they live is kept too strong for Soviet forces to cross the Elbe. Sooner or later the iron curtain will rust away, and by peaceful means Germans to the east of it will join their compatriots in the shelter of the international Union.

The principles of freedom when embodied in institutions too strong for aggressors to challenge have more power to penetrate and a range longer than bullets. Those principles will excite the envy of Russia's satellite States and kindle in them a desire to join the international Union. It is probable that Czechoslovakia will be the first to recover her freedom. As the Union comes to include these States, the ideas on which it is based will find their way into Russia. The Russian masses themselves, envying the freedom of their western neighbours, will grow increasingly impatient of a régime which can only last so long as it is based, as it now is, on slavery. A time will come when they will throw off their chains, learn to govern themselves, and seek membership in the Western Union.

XXII

THE MIDDLE EAST AND OIL

FOR two centuries the Government of India had found it necessary to extend its control to the Persian Gulf. Its first task, to suppress the Arab pirates, was completed in 1820. Its Gulf headquarters was at Bushire on the Persian coast till 1946, when it shifted its base to Bahrein.

In the nineteenth century the Gulf was a sort of pocket, but with the turn of the century the scheme for the Baghdad Railway, projected by the Turks under German inspiration, led Curzon to realize that the Gulf was becoming a vital line of communication between Britain, India, the Far East, Australia, and New Zealand.

In 1908 oil was discovered in Persia. In the first world war Persia became the avenue from India to Mesopotamia through which assistance could be given to the Arabs in their struggle for independence. In the course of that war it became an air route.

By 1939 the oilfields in that region were producing 14,000,000 tons, and in 1948 produced 26,000,000. In the nineteen thirties oil was found in Arabia, and on the Bahrein Islands. These sources are now yielding 30,000,000 tons, and American experts have proved that reserves amount to 3,000,000,000. Reserves round the Persian Gulf are estimated to amount to at least 4,500,000,000.

The oil centre of gravity has thus shifted in the course of this century to the Middle East. Europe, India, the Far East, and America are now largely dependent on oil production in these regions. The wells are controlled by Britain, the U.S.A., Holland, and France. Oil is pumped through a pipe-line to the Mediterranean and other pipe-lines are under construction.

Speaking of Shakespeare, John Masefield wrote that some obsession lies at the root of all his tragedies. He might have added that some obsession lies at the root of all the major tragedies of history. The Marxian obsession of the Russian Communists that war with capitalist States is inevitable is the reason why we have failed, after winning the war in alliance with Russia, to stabilize peace. That war has not yet broken out is due to the fact that Russia dare not embark on war unless she controls the major oil reserves which are in Persia and Arabia, controlled by four capitalist States. She is only 1,000 miles from these resources. The four States that control them are at least 6,000 miles away. The eyes of Russia are on these resources. The strategic centre with which the Western nations are concerned is not Berlin but Arabia and the Persian Gulf. They can prevent war so long, and only so long, as they can all maintain joint control of the oil reserves of the Middle East and the pipe-lines from them to the Mediterranean. The Western nations that own no oil wells there are just as much concerned, because, if a world war broke out, they will all be involved no less than Britain, America, Holland, and France.

In both world wars our strategy in Mesopotamia, Arabia, and Persia was based on India. From that basis was drawn the human and material reinforcements which enabled us to control the Middle East. Now with India and Pakistan as independent States that situation has ceased to exist. We no longer have an anchorage in India from which human and material reinforcement can be drawn.

In order to prevent war, the Western Powers must control the oil reserves of the Middle East, without such anchorage in India as we had till after the last war. Our efforts to build an ersatz basis in East Africa will not enable us to keep our hold on the Persian Gulf, or the Americans, Dutch, and French to keep their hold on their oil wells in Arabia. We must have unity of front in those regions and bases to compensate for those which we have lost in India. Mr. Bevin warned us against such illusions when on December 9, 1948, he said to the House of Commons:

I am against using any promises or façades to lead people to believe that they have something which, when the test comes, does not work. I will not comment on another international institution about the effectiveness of which all of us at the moment are gravely concerned. One other point [Interruption]—Well, the United Nations is giving us grave concern as to whether it is going to face the serious problems involved.

With an issue so tremendous at stake let the Western nations beware of thinking that this difficult and complicated task of protecting their interests in Arabia and Persia can be done by a so-called Western Union which is, in fact, no more than a replica of U.N.O. When an international government is created, responsible to free nations in Western Europe, North America, Australia, and New Zealand, for the task of controlling the oil reserves of the Middle East, then war with the Western Nations will be out of the question for Russia.

XXIII

WHY IT IS IMPORTANT THAT DOMINION STATESMEN SHOULD ATTEND THE CONVENTION

IMPORTANT as it is that British statesmen should take their part in framing the constitution of an international Union it is of even greater importance that Dominion statesmen should attend the International Convention, and pull their weight there. They, even more than British ministers, know how essential it is for Dominion governments to retain control of migration and tariffs. They, better than British ministers, could convince the nations of Western Europe that a union which deprived national States of power to control their own composition and structure could never be joined by democracies overseas.

In the working of federal institutions British ministers are as inexperienced as those of France, Belgium, Holland, or of the Scandinavian States. The Swiss are the only nation in Europe who know how to work them as yet. Of the British Dominions, Canada and Australia have both created and worked federations for themselves. If the governments of the U.S.A. and Switzerland would appoint advisers like Mr. John Foster Dulles and Professor Rappard to help in the task of drawing the first international constitution they would render a service to the whole world as well as to themselves. If once such a union comes into being, I have no doubt that both the U.S.A. and Switzerland will find their way into it, and care should be taken in drawing the constitution to make it easy for them to do so.

At The Hague Conference, Churchill urged that a United Europe must be based on a European patriotism. This was natural at a conference meeting on the continent of Europe. Here the conference was doubtless thinking of the United States of America. In private discussion the idea that the bond uniting the nations of Europe was the fact that they lived on the same continent was questioned by Professor Rappard. In his view, separate nations are held together by common principles of life expressed in their institutions. This explains why we feel a closer relation with communities on the other side of the world like Canada, South Africa, Australia, and New Zealand than we feel with nations of Europe which are almost within sight of our eyes. It also explains why the peoples of Western and Eastern Europe, with no natural frontier between them, are divided in a way which threatens the peace of the world.

If Western Union is to become the nucleus of a world Commonwealth it must be realized that the bond which unites free peoples is their common freedom which they must unite to defend. An attack on one by a despotism is an attack on all. For democracies there is now no place for neutrality. If once France or Britain are attacked, the freedom of Canada, Australia, New Zealand, or South Africa is as much at stake as that of Belgium, Holland, Denmark, Norway, or Sweden.

It is for this reason that no Dominion can afford to stand out of the first international Union. Those who join in framing its constitution will realize this in the course of their task. At present Dominion ministers can insist that they are not committed to war by anything which the British Government may do in foreign affairs. They are always informed and consulted on every point, but none the less they know in their hearts that final decisions must all be left to the British Government. They also believe (and rightly) that the British Government will leave no doubt in the minds of aggressors that any attack on any Dominion will be treated as an attack on Britain herself. Every Dominion knows that any attack on them, or by them, would involve the United Kingdom in war.

This situation would be greatly modified when the conduct of foreign affairs for the British Commonwealth passed from Downing Street to the federal government of the Union. Such a government, responsible to the nations of Europe for their common defence, would not be able to inform and consult any Dominion governments, which were unwilling to accept responsibility in advance, on details of policy from day to day. On the other hand, if that policy should lead to war those Dominions would be drawn into it as certainly as they would be to-day if the policy of the British Government led to war. The unreality of their situation would then be forced upon them. They would find that they were in fact satellite States, but without the privilege of previous information and consultation which they now have in the British Commonwealth.

All this would become plain to their representatives in advance if they joined with the governments of Western Europe in the task of shaping a system in which the democracies could unite for the common defence of their free institutions and way of life. Their co-operation in this preliminary task will not commit their governments or electorates in any way. But it will ensure that the first international constitution is so framed that oversea countries can when they choose add their military strength and their great industrial resources to those of the free nations in Europe. If the British and especially the Dominion governments hold aloof from the task of framing the first constitution of an international Commonwealth the result will be disastrous to the future of mankind.

Americans, like Washington, Hamilton, and Madison, who played a leading part in the Philadelphia Convention were mainly responsible for the fact that the Constitution worked when it came into operation. It is obvious that when the first international Commonwealth has come into being, the men who have taken a leading part in framing its provisions will be called upon to administer them. The first federal ministries must largely be drawn from such men. One trembles to think of an international Commonwealth in the government of which no Anglo-Saxon statesmen were taking a part.

How is it that our ministers hesitate to support demands of France and Belgium that immediate steps should be taken to unite Western Europe? The main reason, I think, is that States in Western Europe have not got the English Channel and the North Sea between them and armies which might at any moment overwhelm them from the East. They have known what slavery is. We have not.

A subsidiary reason may be that the governments of the smaller democracies in the Benelux group are not so preoccupied as our over-burdened ministers and

M

have had time to survey the problem involved in the World Revolution as a whole. If only our ministers could have such a survey before them they would be surprised to find that the difficulties from which they are now shrinking are not so formidable as their permanent advisers have led them to believe. There is nothing which so braces the mind as the naked facts. They would see how all the secondary problems could be handled more easily and brought to solution when once the world was relieved from the nightmare of war. They might also realize how utterly precarious is such work as they are able to do so long as the drift to a third war goes on. As it is they are tied hand and foot in the toils of a system which imposes on men in office a greater burden than human shoulders can carry. If, in result, we drift again into war, all their measures of social reform, and all the plans they have laid for meeting our debts, for stabilizing currency, for reviving production in all its forms will vanish in one great conflagration. Nothing but dust and ashes will be left.

XXIV

THAT IMMORTAL GARLAND

O N January 11, 1949, at the Rolls Royce works in Derby, a window in memory of the pilots who risked and gave their lives in the Battle of Britain was unveiled by Lord Tedder, Marshal of the Royal Air Force. His speech recalls what Dr. Benjamin Rush had said of the American Revolution in 1787:

> In the Battle of Britain our pilots did their utmost. Were we doing all that we had in us for the faith, beliefs, and ideals for which Britain stood? It was a very real challenge, for history was painted on a rather larger canvas than most of us realized. The Battle of Britain, Alamein, and even the surrender of Germany and Italy were not the ultimate victory. *That victory for the faith in which we believed was not yet; it had still to be won.* We prayed that it might be won without recourse again to arms, but we should achieve it only by displaying the spirit which inspired those men in 1940.

Here is one who played his part in winning the war who dedicates himself to winning the peace, as Washington and the men who fought in the American war had done. Oliver Wendel Holmes said, 'Everything that is worth doing has been done by mutual admiration societies'. What society was ever more entitled to mutual admiration than the Royal Air Force? The fighters who know what war means are foremost in the task of ending it once for all. As Mrs. Marshall says in her wonderful book:

> Why should a soldier want war? He certainly knows the horrors of it. Does a fireman want fires? Do the police want crime? Their whole training and duty is to protect us from these ills. Why then is it not the soldier's idea of duty to protect us from wars? Certainly it is, and has always been, General Marshall's paramount desire. His answer to the opposition was short and direct: 'As history has repeatedly proved, it is not with the brass hats but with the brass heads that the danger to our country lies.' (*Together, Annals of an Army Wife*, by Katherine Tupper Marshall, p. 184. Published by the Blandford Press, London.)

In the words we have quoted, Lord Tedder was saying to us what Dr. Benjamin Rush was saying to Americans one hundred and fifty years ago. They make us see that the American Revolution was only the first act in the drama of the World Revolution. Washington divined this, and so had Benjamin Franklin when on October 22, 1787, he wrote to Ferdinand Grand, his friend in Paris:

> I send you enclos'd the propos'd new Federal Constitution for these States. . . . If it succeeds, I do not see why you might not in Europe carry the project of good Henry the 4th into execution, by forming a Federal Union, and one Grand Republick of all its different States and Kingdoms, by means of a like Convention, for we had many interests to reconcile.

As Lord Tedder says, the men who fought the Battle of Britain were giving their lives for a faith in the freedom which their fathers won for us step by step. That freedom was handed on as a gift to mankind, and the nations who accepted the gift united with us to preserve it. They are now looking to us to show them how to establish our common freedom on a footing so firm that no aggressor will ever dare to challenge it again. In all history no such call has ever been made to leaders of men than is now being made to our present rulers. Never has this country, nor any other, had so splendid a chance to render a service to all mankind. Our thoughts revert to the story how the interpreter took the pilgrims journeying to the City of God 'into a room where was a man that could look no way but downwards, with a muck-rake in his hand. There stood, also, one over his head with a celestial crown in his hand, and proffered him that crown for his muck-rake; but the man did neither look up nor regard but raked to himself the straws, the small sticks and the dust of the floor.'

Freedom is the crown held over our heads—the freedom that we have done so much to create, but have still to complete, by transferring the task of preserving it from sovereign governments to the people themselves.

In the last century Lord Acton, the greatest prophet that Liberals have ever had, said that as democracies approached adult suffrage, the mandate of liberalism, so far as social and domestic questions are concerned, would exhaust itself. The future of liberalism would then lie in the international field, and in that field it must take the form of international federation. The Liberal Party were deaf to his warning. They took the position that national sovereignty is the final expression of Liberal principles, and so identified liberalism with nationalism. Their influence was thrown not merely into the maintenance of national sovereignties, but into their multiplication. These ideas inspired the Treaty of Versailles and the Covenant of the League. One result may be seen in the present position of the Liberal Party in this country.

A similar warning has come to their successors who are now in office from Walter Lippmann (see page 86). Will British ministers heed this American warning? Will they consider in time whether the fate that has overtaken liberalism may not be in store for Labour? Will they know the day of their visitation and put their hand to the task of carrying freedom towards its final completion?

In the mind of the Liberal Party the conception of liberalism was limited to the extension of the franchise to every man and woman of age. The importance of giving the voters an ever increasing responsibility was overlooked. They failed to see that voters cannot be responsible for decisions so long as they have to make too many decisions in casting one vote.

This truth can be seen if we think what would have happened if in 1945 there could have been two elections, one for domestic and another for external affairs. If electors had had first to think only of the best government to inaugurate social reforms, they would, I believe, have given the Labour a bigger majority than it got. If at another election they had been free to say who were the men to win and preserve the peace they would probably have entrusted the task to the ministers who had won the war against terrible odds.

The responsibility of electors is fatally limited so long as at general elections they have with a single vote to choose one government to handle domestic affairs and also the issues of peace and war. Electorates cannot be made really responsible for both these vital functions until they are allowed to choose one set of men for domestic affairs and another set of men to deal with the issues of peace and war. Not till we do what Americans did in 1787 can a real responsibility for all public affairs be laid on the shoulders of the people themselves. That is the crown that is held above us. How long must we cling to our muck-rake and 'slink out of the race, where that immortal garland which is to be run for, not without dust and heat' has to be won? Another poet has written our answer.

> It is not to be thought of that the flood
> Of British freedom, which, to the open sea
> Of the world's praise, from dark antiquity
> Hath flowed, 'with pomp of waters, unwithstood,'
> Roused though it be full often to a mood
> Which spurns the check of salutary bands,
> That this most famous Stream in bogs and sands
> Should perish; and to evil and to good
> Be lost for ever. In our halls is hung
> Armoury of the invincible knights of old:
> We must be free or die, who speak the tongue
> That Shakespeare spoke; the faith and morals hold
> Which Milton held.—In everything we are sprung
> Of Earth's first blood, have titles manifold.